the GIFT of Rest

40 SIMPLE INVITATIONS TO RECLAIM YOUR PEACE AND PURPOSE

DR. RENEE SUNDAY, M.D

Copyright © 2025 – All rights reserved.

No part of this publication may be reproduced, distributed, or transmitted in any form or by any means, including photocopying, recording, or other electronic or mechanical methods, without the prior written permission of the publisher, except in the case of brief quotations embodied in critical reviews and certain other noncommercial uses permitted by copyright law.

I. Introduction..4
- *Why You've Been Restless*
- *The Birth of the REST Framework*
- *How to Use This Book*
- *A Personal Invitation to Pause*

II. 40 Simple Invitations to Reclaim Your Peace & Purpose 4
- *Part I — R: REFLECTION*
- *Part II — E: ENVIRONMENT*
- *Part III — S: STILLNESS*
- *Part IV — T: TIME*

III. About the Author 4

IV. Notes 4

INTRODUCTION

Introduction

When was the last time you truly rested?

Not the kind of rest that happens when you're forced to stop. I mean a deep, life-giving rest — the kind that quiets your thoughts, soothes your soul, and reminds your body that it's safe to breathe again.

For years, I confused motion with meaning. I wore busyness like a badge. From the operating room to the pulpit, from coaching sessions to media appearances, I was moving — always moving. Productive, yes. Purposeful, sometimes. But rested? Not at all.

Then God got my attention.

INTRODUCTION

It wasn't a collapse or a crisis. It was a whisper.

A clear, still instruction:
 "Rest."

At first, I pushed back. "Lord, I have people depending on me."

But He responded, *"And I have something to say — but you won't hear Me until you slow down."*

INTRODUCTION

This Is Your Wake-Up Call

In our culture, rest is often mistaken for weakness. We think rest means giving up, stepping back, or losing our edge. But what if rest isn't about inactivity — it's about alignment?

Rest isn't where purpose goes to die. It's where clarity comes alive.

The moment I stopped chasing and started listening, I realized that I had been doing so much for God that I hadn't been still *with* Him. That's what this book is about — not just recovering energy, but recovering your *focus* and *faith*.

INTRODUCTION

What This Book Is
(And What It's Not)

This is not a book about escaping. It's not about zoning out or checking out.

This is a book about tuning *in*.

It's about making space — in your schedule, your spirit, and your surroundings — so you can *receive* again.

Not just sleep more. Not just say no.

But actually return to a way of living where you move from peace, not pressure.

INTRODUCTION

Inside, you'll find 40 simple practices based on my REST Framework:

- **R – Reflection:** Listen deeply. Think clearly.

- **E – Environment:** Set the atmosphere for calm.

- **S – Stillness:** Be fully present, without guilt.

- **T – Time:** Honor divine timing over deadlines.

Each practice is short, doable, and real — something you can apply whether you're in the carpool lane or leading a team meeting. And every one of them is designed to help you step into your day from a place of clarity, not chaos.

INTRODUCTION

Rest Isn't Optional — It's Instruction

Exodus 33:14 says, *"My Presence will go with you, and I will give you rest."*

That's not a suggestion. It's a promise. It's an assignment.

Rest is a faith move. It's a bold declaration that God's presence is enough. That you don't have to prove your worth through your performance. That your best work comes from your anchored self, not your anxious one.

INTRODUCTION

How to Use This Book

You can read this book front to back or skip to what your soul needs today.

Each practice includes:

- *A short reflection or real-life story*
- *A simple action you can take*
- *An encouragement to keep you grounded*
- *A journal or prayer prompt to help it sink in*

Go at your own pace. Linger where God speaks. Repeat the ones that hit home.

INTRODUCTION

A Final Word Before You Begin

Y ou don't need another planner.
　You don't need more pressure.
　You need rest that restores — mind, body, and spirit.

My prayer is that this book becomes your quiet space in a loud world. A pause in the scroll. A breath between responsibilities. A reminder that God is not in the rush — He's in the rest.

Welcome back to yourself.

Let's begin.

— *Dr. Renee Sunday, M.D.*

INTRODUCTION

A Personal Invitation to Pause

This book is more than pages and practices —
it's your moment to pause without guilt.

To listen again.

To return to the rhythm of grace that has
always been calling you home.

Let's begin.

— Dr. Renee Sunday, M.D.

40
Simple Invitations To Reclaim Your
Peace & Purpose

PART I
Reflection

MAKE ROOM FOR GOD'S VOICE
Stillness begins with honesty. This is where clarity grows.

PART I: REFLECTION

INVITATION 01:

The Check-In —
"How Am I, Really?"

"Rest begins when you stop
pretending you're fine."

We say "I'm fine" so quickly that we don't even hear the lie anymore. We say it to others. We say it to ourselves. Sometimes, we even say it to God. But fine doesn't mean whole. And rest doesn't happen until honesty does.

I remember standing in a room full of people, giving advice, encouraging others, showing up strong. And yet inside, I felt empty. Not burnt out — just hollow. That was the moment I realized I hadn't checked in with *me* in a long time. I was living on auto-pilot, not alignment. Pouring out wisdom with an empty well. My calendar looked full, but my soul was

PART I: REFLECTION

quiet — too quiet. And that silence wasn't peace; it was neglect.

Checking in with yourself may sound simple, but it's one of the most courageous things you can do. Because if you're not careful, life will keep handing you roles to play, masks to wear, and expectations to meet — all while your soul quietly whispers, "I miss you."

Sometimes we avoid checking in because we're afraid of what we'll find. We're afraid the truth will overwhelm us. Or that if we stop moving, everything will fall apart. But the truth doesn't come to crush you. It comes to *free* you. You can't find rest if you're still pretending you're okay. And God? He doesn't bless the polished version of you. He blesses the honest one. He meets you in the real, raw places — not the rehearsed ones.

There's a reason Psalm 139:23 says, *"Search me, O God, and know my heart; test me and know my anxious thoughts."* That prayer is a check-in. It's saying, "God, I don't even know what's in here anymore. But You do. And I trust You to hold it."

You might be juggling a hundred things. You may have people depending on you. But here's what I need you to know: **you are worth pausing for.** Not because you've accomplished everything. Not because you've finally earned rest. But because your soul matters. And you are not called to ignore yourself in the name of serving others.

PART I: REFLECTION

This invitation isn't a productivity hack. It's not another task to check off. This is your soul's chance to speak up and be heard — by you, and by the One who created you.

The Invitation:

Take five minutes today. No phone. No noise. No mask. Sit with a pen and paper and ask yourself:

"How am I, really?"

Write what comes. Don't edit. Don't judge. Let the words come honestly, even if they don't make sense yet. The page is your space — a sacred conversation between your heart and Heaven.

Why This Matters:

You can't rest from what you haven't named. And what stays unspoken will eventually surface — usually through stress, anxiety, or burnout.

But when you pause and listen, you shift from being driven to being led. That's where rest begins — not in the absence of activity, but in the presence of truth.

PART I: REFLECTION

Journal Prompt:

🦋 What emotions have I been ignoring lately?

_____
_____
_____
_____

🦋 What is one word that honestly describes how I feel today?

_____
_____
_____
_____

🦋 What would I tell God right now if I stopped pretending?

_____
_____
_____
_____

PART I: REFLECTION

God's Promises to Carry With You:

"The Lord is near to all who call on Him, to all who call on Him in truth." — Psalm 145:18 (NIV)

"Come to Me, all who are weary and burdened, and I will give you rest." — Matthew 11:28 (NIV)

Your Rest Word:

Permission

PART I: REFLECTION

INVITATION 02:

Pour and Pray —
"Emptying Out is a Holy Act"

*"God already knows. He's just
waiting on you to bring it to Him."*

There's a kind of exhaustion that sleep can't fix — the kind that comes from carrying what you were never meant to hold. And sometimes, we don't even realize how much we've been carrying until we let it out.

I once walked into my prayer closet and didn't say anything for five minutes. My heart was full, but not in the way we use that phrase when we're happy. It was full of questions. Full of thoughts I didn't want to say out loud. Full of emotions I had tried to manage on my own. And the Lord said to me, gently, "Pour."

PART I: REFLECTION

Not "perform." Not "pretend." Just — pour.

That moment changed how I pray. I realized that prayer isn't always about poetic language or perfect posture. Sometimes it's groaning. Sometimes it's tears. Sometimes it's just sitting with God and saying, "I don't even have words, but I know You hear me."

When we come to Him full of frustration, disappointment, doubt, or fatigue — and still choose to pour it out at His feet — that is rest in action. That is surrender. And that is worship.

The Invitation:

Find a private space — a room, a car, even the bathroom if needed. Close the door and say everything to God that you've been carrying in silence. Speak it. Cry it. Write it. Whatever form it takes, let it out.

If you're not sure where to begin, start with this:

"Lord, I haven't said this out loud, but..."

Then finish the sentence.

PART I: REFLECTION

Why This Matters:

What you don't release will remain buried. And buried things don't disappear — they surface later as anxiety, impatience, or disconnection. When you pour it out, you're not informing God — you're inviting Him to step in. And in that space, He can replace the heaviness with peace.

Journal Prompt:

🦋 What am I trying to carry alone?

_____
_____
_____
_____

🦋 What's one thing I haven't brought to God because it feels too messy?

_____
_____
_____
_____

PART I: REFLECTION

🦋 How did I feel after letting it out?

_____

_____

_____

_____

God's Promises to Carry With You:

"Cast your cares on the Lord and He will sustain you; He will never let the righteous be shaken." — Psalm 55:22 (NIV)

"Before they call I will answer; while they are still speaking I will hear." — Isaiah 65:24 (NIV)

Inviting God into your daily rhythms, the more those rhythms become restful.

Your Rest Word: *Release*

PART I: REFLECTION

INVITATION 03:

Boxes and Breakthrough —
"Let The Ordinary Calm You"

> *"Sometimes peace finds you while*
> *your hands are busy."*

We often look for rest in grand gestures — a weekend off, a long nap, or some big breakthrough. But often, rest finds us right in the middle of what looks like a mess. A pile of boxes. A moment of transition. A task we'd rather skip.

I was in the middle of cleaning out my storage room — and it wasn't cute. Dust, bins, half-labeled boxes filled with everything from old journals to expired products. I had pushed that chore to the back burner for months. The plan was to declutter. But God had other plans.

PART I: REFLECTION

As I pulled out box after box, I started seeing my own life mirrored back at me — things I held onto "just in case," items from past seasons I'd outgrown but hadn't released.

Some boxes were filled with memories. Others, with reminders of dreams I hadn't pursued. I started feeling the weight — not just physically, but emotionally. And then came the whisper:

"Let go. Make room. I'm doing something new."

That's when I knew this wasn't just about cleaning. This was a *spiritual detox.*

Every item I threw out felt like I was releasing something else — guilt, fear, regret, even false responsibility. I didn't cry because of the stuff. I cried because God was working through the stuff.

That storage room turned into an altar. And those boxes became breakthroughs.

PART I: REFLECTION

The Invitation:

Find one box — physical or symbolic — that's been tucked away too long. It could be a storage bin, a junk drawer, an old bag. As you go through it, pay attention to what emotions surface. What do you really need to keep? What are you ready to release?

Before you start, pray:

"God, help me make room for what You're doing next."

Let the process be slow. Let it speak to you. Let it stir up things that need to go — not just in your hands, but in your heart.

Why This Matters:

We carry more than we realize. Emotional clutter builds up just like physical clutter does.

But when you create space — even in a box — you make room to breathe again. You make room for clarity. You make room for rest.

PART I: REFLECTION

Journal Prompt:

- What am I holding onto that represents an old version of me?

- What am I afraid to let go of — and why?

- What would I gain if I finally made space for peace?

PART I: REFLECTION

God's Promises to Carry With You:

"Forget the former things; do not dwell on the past. See, I am doing a new thing!" — Isaiah 43:18–19 (NIV)

"Come to Me, all who are weary and burdened, and I will give you rest." — Matthew 11:28 (NIV)

Your Rest Word: Space

PART I: REFLECTION

INVITATION 04:

*The Thought Journal —
"Every Thought Doesn't Deserve
to Stay"*

"Rest starts in the mind. And some
thoughts need to be evicted."

Sometimes the loudest thing keeping us from rest isn't our schedule — it's our thinking. We're bombarded all day long: internal conversations, outside opinions, false narratives, future scenarios. It's no wonder we can't hear from God — our minds are full of noise that doesn't belong.

There was a season when my mind was racing constantly. I wasn't anxious — I was overstimulated. I'd go to bed tired

PART I: REFLECTION

but still wide awake, mentally sorting through conversations, projects, fears, and even things I hadn't faced yet. One night, I asked God, "Why am I so unsettled?" And He responded with one word:
"Inventory."

I knew exactly what He meant. Not a spiritual retreat. Not another sermon. He wanted me to take inventory of my thoughts — not just the ones I was aware of, but the ones I had been allowing to run wild without challenge.

So I grabbed a notebook and began to write. Every thought that surfaced, I wrote it down. The kind ones. The mean ones. The fearful ones. The repetitive ones. Then I went back, line by line, and asked one question:

"Is this from God, or is this something I've just been tolerating?"

That's when everything shifted.

You don't have to believe every thought you think. And you don't have to accept every thought that shows up in your head. God gave us the ability to take thoughts captive — but that begins with awareness. If your mind is the battlefield, the journal is your weapon.

PART I: REFLECTION

The Invitation:

Set aside ten minutes today. Open a journal or digital note and write down your thoughts freely — no filter. Let them pour out as they come: worries, hopes, lies, to-do lists, random fears. Then go back and circle the ones that are not aligned with peace, truth, or grace.

Afterward, pray:

"Lord, renew my mind. Help me make space for what's true."

You can even write a scripture next to each lie. This isn't therapy — it's soul training.

Why This Matters:

Unchecked thoughts don't go away — they grow. They become patterns. And patterns become strongholds. But the moment you start questioning what doesn't belong, you make space for what does: peace, clarity, and divine instruction.

Writing it out doesn't just clear your mind — it retrains it.

PART I: REFLECTION

Journal Prompt:

🦋 What thoughts keep repeating in my mind that don't align with peace?

🦋 Where did these thoughts come from — a voice, a memory, an assumption?

🦋 What is God's truth in place of those thoughts?

PART I: REFLECTION

God's Promises to Carry With You:

"Do not conform to the pattern of this world, but be transformed by the renewing of your mind." — Romans 12:2 (NIV)

"We take captive every thought to make it obedient to Christ." — 2 Corinthians 10:5 (NIV)

Your Rest Word: Clarity

PART I: REFLECTION

INVITATION 05:

Look at Your Yeses —
"Peace Comes with Boundaries"

> *"Rest isn't just about saying no —*
> *it's about revisiting what you've*
> *already said yes to."*

Many of us don't feel tired because we're doing too much. We feel tired because we're doing too much of the wrong things — things God never told us to pick up. And sometimes, the weight we're carrying isn't from disobedience — it's from well-intentioned yeses that are now silently draining us.

I remember reviewing my calendar and realizing how busy it looked — but how burdened I felt. Most of those

PART I: REFLECTION

appointments were things I agreed to. Projects I said yes to.

Conversations I made room for. Commitments I prayed over but didn't always pause long enough to discern. And that's when the Holy Spirit nudged me:
"Your yes is holy. Guard it."

That word stopped me.

I had been so used to helping, serving, showing up, and filling gaps — that I forgot my yes was a seed. Every yes grows something. Some grow fruit. Some grow frustration. And when your yes is scattered everywhere, your peace gets diluted.

So I sat down and wrote out everything I had committed to in that season. I asked two questions for each one:
"Did God assign this to me?"
"Is this still life-giving or just lingering?"

I was surprised at how many things had expired — but I was still carrying them like they were fresh instructions.

PART I: REFLECTION

The Invitation:

Pull out your planner, digital calendar, or task list. Write down everything you've said yes to this week or month — from major commitments to small tasks. Then pray over each one.

Ask:

- *Did God assign this to me?*
- *Am I still graced for this?*
- *Is this producing peace or pressure?*

If you feel a release, it may be time to set it down. That doesn't mean you're quitting — it means you're realigning.

Why This Matters:

Every yes has a cost. And if you don't evaluate where your yeses are going, you'll spend your energy in places God never called you to invest. Boundaries aren't walls — they're wisdom. They're how we honor our assignment and protect our rest.

This isn't about being selfish. It's about being strategic. The right yes is powerful. The wrong one is draining.

PART I: REFLECTION

Journal Prompt:

🦋 God is leading me?

🦋 What "good thing" is actually crowding out my peace?

🦋 Where is God asking me to reclaim space in my life?

PART I: REFLECTION

God's Promises to Carry With You:

"Let your 'Yes' be 'Yes,' and your 'No,' 'No'; anything more comes from the evil one." — Matthew 5:37 (NIV)

"The blessing of the Lord makes rich, and He adds no sorrow with it." — Proverbs 10:22 (ESV)

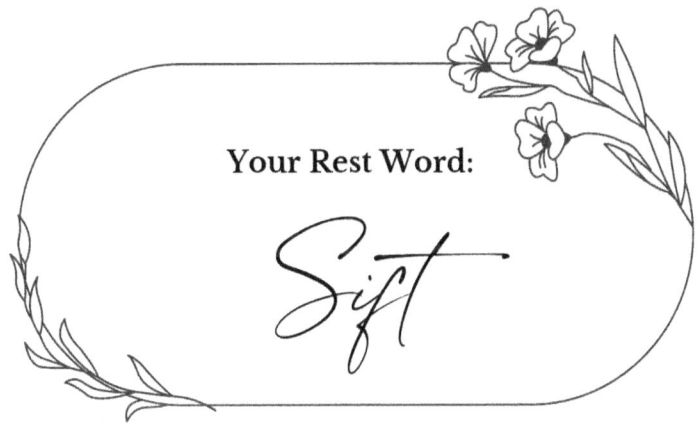

Your Rest Word: Sift

Let God sift your yeses. Keep what's assigned.
Release what's expired.

PART I: REFLECTION

INVITATION 06:

The Whisper Walk —
"Stillness Will Show You What
Noise Has Hidden"

"When you walk in silence, you
start to hear what matters most."

It's easy to forget how loud life can be. The buzzing notifications, the phone calls, the background TV, the unspoken pressure to always be on. We live in a world where silence is rare — and almost uncomfortable. But there's something sacred about a moment without sound. That's where you start to feel again. That's where God whispers.

I used to fill every quiet moment. Music, phone calls,

PART I: REFLECTION

podcasts — even worship music. I had convinced myself I needed noise to feel motivated. But I began to notice something: even with all the "positive" noise, I still felt foggy. Disconnected. Drained.

One day, I left my phone in the house and stepped outside — no earbuds, no agenda, just a walk. That's when I realized how much I had been missing. The rhythm of my own breath. The crunch of gravel under my feet. The way the trees moved like they had something to say. I wasn't just moving through the world — I was finally *with* it.

And that's when I heard the whisper:
"I've been waiting for this stillness."

Tears filled my eyes. Not because I was sad — but because I hadn't realized how deeply I needed quiet. Not empty quiet — but *intentional stillness*. The kind that heals. The kind that lets buried thoughts rise and distractions fall away.

That's what I now call my *Whisper Walk*. It's not a workout. It's not multitasking. It's not time to talk. It's space for God to speak.

PART I: REFLECTION

The Invitation:

Choose one walk this week — even if it's just five or ten minutes. Leave your phone behind or turn it on silent. Don't listen to music or a podcast. Just walk.
Let your surroundings speak. Let God speak. Don't force it — just receive it.

And before you begin, whisper this prayer:

"God, meet me in this stillness. Let me hear what I've been missing."

You may hear something. You may feel a release. You may cry. Or you may simply notice a tree you've passed a hundred times without seeing. Either way, it's holy ground.

Why This Matters:

We don't often realize how cluttered our thoughts have become until we get quiet enough to hear them clearly.

Stillness isn't passive — it's powerful. It reveals the condition of your soul. It uncovers what's been buried. It brings God's voice back into focus.

PART I: REFLECTION

 You were never meant to live on autopilot. There are insights you've missed because life has been too loud.

This isn't about being less productive. It's about being more present — so your rest can be rooted, not rushed.

Practical Encouragement:

If walking outside isn't available, do a Whisper Walk inside your home — walk slowly from room to room. Open the blinds. Feel the floor under your feet. Ask God, "What are You highlighting today?"

Your walk might become a prayer. Or a memory may resurface that needs healing. Don't judge what comes up. Just walk it out with God.

You don't need a mountain. You need a moment. That's enough.

Journal Prompt:

What thoughts surface when there's no noise?

_____

_____

_____

_____

PART I: REFLECTION

🦋 What did I notice during my Whisper Walk that I normally overlook?

_____
_____
_____
_____
_____

🦋 What did God show me or remind me of in the stillness?

_____
_____
_____
_____
_____

God's Promises to Carry With You:

"In returning and rest you shall be saved; in quietness and in trust shall be your strength." — Isaiah 30:15 (ESV)

"Be still, and know that I am God." — Psalm 46:10 (NIV)

PART I: REFLECTION

Your Rest Word:
Tune

Tune your heart to God's whisper.
The silence holds sound you've been missing.

PART I: REFLECTION

INVITATION 07:

Declutter with Grace —
"Clearing Space for the Spirit to Breathe"

"Peace doesn't live in clutter.
Grace needs room to move."

I stood in the hallway with a half-full trash bag in one hand and a box of items labeled "keep...maybe" in the other. I was trying to clean a room, but what I uncovered was far deeper. It wasn't just physical clutter. It was emotional weight I didn't know I was still carrying.

Old books from a past season. Notebooks filled with ideas I never pursued. Gifts from people no longer in my life.

PART I: REFLECTION

And then it hit me:
Why am I still holding on to what I've outgrown?

That's when the Holy Spirit whispered:
  "Grace breathes best in open spaces."

I exhaled — not just from the task, but from the revelation. Clutter isn't just stuff on the floor. It's the buildup of unmade decisions. The "just in case" items. The guilt-laced objects. The reminders of what didn't work out.

And even when the clutter seems harmless, it takes up space that your peace and purpose were meant to occupy.

Sometimes, rest looks like a room that breathes.

Sometimes, healing begins with a trash bag.

PART I: REFLECTION

The Invitation:

Choose one drawer, one shelf, or one corner of a room — somewhere that has been calling for your attention but hasn't gotten it. Take a breath. Ask God to meet you in the process.

As you sort, ask these questions:

- *Does this still reflect who I am becoming?*
- *Am I keeping this out of guilt, fear, or avoidance?*
- *Is this blessing me or blocking me?*

Let yourself release without shame. Let grace be your guide.

This isn't about minimalism. It's about ministry — the kind that happens in your soul when your surroundings no longer speak of confusion or chaos.

PART I: REFLECTION

Why This Matters:

We serve a God of order. He created spaciousness, beauty, and intentionality. When our lives are overflowing with clutter — physical or emotional — it's harder to hear, harder to focus, and harder to rest.

Decluttering with grace means you release what no longer fits the season you're in. It doesn't mean it wasn't useful before — it just means you're making room for what God is doing now.

And here's the truth: You don't need to keep something to honor the memory. You don't have to hold on to a thing to value the lesson. Sometimes the release is the honor.

Practical Encouragement:

Set a 20-minute timer. That's it. You don't need a full day or a perfect plan. Pick one space, say a short prayer, and begin.

Speak this aloud:
"God, I give You this space. Help me let go with grace."

You might cry. You might laugh. You might just feel relief. All are welcome in this moment. Let the act be part of your rest.

And when you're done — sit for a few minutes. Look at the space you cleared. Thank God for the fresh start. Even small shifts prepare the heart for big breakthroughs.

PART I: REFLECTION

Journal Prompt:

🦋 What emotions rise when I think about letting go of certain items or habits?

_____
_____
_____
_____

🦋 What areas in my life feel too crowded or chaotic — physically, mentally, or spiritually?

_____
_____
_____
_____
_____

🦋 Where is God inviting me to make room?

_____
_____
_____
_____

PART I: REFLECTION

God's Promises to Carry With You:

"Forget the former things; do not dwell on the past. See, I am doing a new thing!" — Isaiah 43:18–19 (NIV)

"Let all things be done decently and in order." — 1 Corinthians 14:40 (KJV)

Your Rest Word: Clear

Clear the room. Clear the weight.
Clear the way for peace to breathe.

PART I: REFLECTION

INVITATION 08:

*Rest Your Mind —
"When Your Thoughts Are
Tired, So Is Your Body"*

> "Mental clutter drains the soul just
> as much as physical clutter drains
> the home."

There are days when it's not your body that's tired — it's your thoughts. You've been thinking, rethinking, overthinking. Wondering if you're doing enough, being enough, showing up enough. The weight isn't always visible, but it's heavy.

PART I: REFLECTION

Rest doesn't start with the body — it starts with the mind. When your mind is racing, everything else follows. Even if you're sitting still, the tension in your shoulders, the pressure behind your eyes, the uneasiness in your stomach — it's all evidence that your mind needs rest too.

This kind of fatigue is subtle. It doesn't show up as sleepiness. It shows up as irritability, forgetfulness, indecision, or emotional numbness. You find yourself staring at the same task for hours. Or waking up more tired than when you went to bed.

I've been there. Some days I could barely hear my own voice underneath all the noise — my to-do list, the expectations of others, the swirl of unanswered questions. I wasn't physically busy, but mentally I was exhausted. And God gently reminded me:

"You're allowed to stop thinking for a moment."

It was simple. But revolutionary.

Resting your mind isn't irresponsible. It's healing.

You don't have to solve it all right now.
You don't have to carry what isn't yours.
And you certainly don't have to rehearse what God has already redeemed.

PART I: REFLECTION

The Invitation:

Give your mind permission to breathe. Take five minutes — no agenda, no goals — just pause.

Here are a few ways to do this:

- Sit with your eyes closed and focus only on your breathing.

- Write down every single thought in your head — no editing, just get it out.

- Place your hand over your heart and whisper,

    "God, I give You what I can't carry."

This isn't about clearing your mind of everything. It's about creating space for peace to enter.

Let your thoughts settle like dust in a quiet room.

PART I: REFLECTION

Why This Matters:

We often underestimate how much our thoughts control our experience of life. A restless mind makes even peaceful moments feel chaotic. But when the mind finds stillness, even a busy season can feel manageable.

God calls us to renew our minds not exhaust them.

He invites us to shift from self-driven problem solving into Spirit-led rest.

Mental rest opens the door for divine clarity.
And clarity births peace.

Journal Prompt:

🌸 What thoughts keep playing on repeat in my mind?

_____

_____

_____

_____

_____

PART I: REFLECTION

🦋 What am I trying to control that God is asking me to release?

🦋 When was the last time I let my mind simply be — without problem-solving or planning?

🦋 How can I invite more mental stillness into my day-to-day rhythm?

PART I: REFLECTION

God's Promises to Carry With You:

"You will keep in perfect peace those whose minds are steadfast, because they trust in You." — Isaiah 26:3 (NIV)

"Come to Me, all who are weary and burdened, and I will give you rest." — Matthew 11:28 (NIV)

Your Rest Word: Quiet

Quiet your thoughts so God's voice has room to rise.

PART I: REFLECTION

INVITATION 09:

The Courage to Pause

*"Even Strength
Needs Stillness"*

There's a quiet kind of courage we don't talk about often.

Not the kind that charges into a new project. Not the kind that pushes through the pain. But the kind that stops... even when everything in you says, "Keep going."

It takes courage to pause.

In a world that celebrates nonstop motion, choosing to rest can feel like weakness. Like laziness. Like giving up. But here's what the Spirit whispered to me one day when I was

PART I: REFLECTION

moving too fast to feel:

"Even the strong must sit."

I didn't want to hear that. Because strong had become my identity. Strong for others. Strong for my brand. Strong in my belief. But inside? I was brittle. Dry. Out of rhythm.

We're not built to sprint forever. Even Jesus paused. He stepped away to pray. He withdrew from the crowds. He rested.

What makes you think you're not allowed to?

Sometimes the most obedient thing you can do is slow down before the crash. **Rest is not a reward for finishing everything. It's part of how you finish well.**

PART I: REFLECTION

The Invitation:

Today, pause — even if it feels unnatural. Not after the email. Not after the groceries. Not when you've earned it. Now.

Pause to ask yourself:

- *Am I running out of habit or instruction?*
- *Is this pace God-ordained or self-imposed?*
- *Have I mistaken constant motion for progress?*

Stillness is where strength is replenished. You don't pause because you're weak — you pause because you're wise.

Why This Matters:

Our culture glorifies exhaustion and calls it excellence. But God never asked you to hustle for His approval. He asked you to walk with Him.

When you pause, you give your soul time to recalibrate. And when your soul is rested, you hear Him more clearly. You move with grace, not grind. And you remember: **rest is a discipline, not a delay.**

PART I: REFLECTION

Journal Prompt:

🦋 What part of my life needs a pause right now?

_____
_____
_____
_____

🦋 Where have I confused strength with striving?

_____
_____
_____
_____
_____

🦋 How does it feel to give myself permission to stop?

_____
_____
_____
_____

PART I: REFLECTION

🦋 What might I hear from God if I were quiet long enough to listen?

_____
_____
_____
_____

God's Promises to Carry With You:

"In returning and rest you shall be saved; in quietness and in trust shall be your strength." — Isaiah 30:15 (ESV)

"Be still, and know that I am God." — Psalm 46:10 (KJV)

Your Rest Word: *Still*

Stillness is not a stop—it's a stance of trust.

PART I: REFLECTION

INVITATION 10:

Boundaries Are Not Betrayal

*"It's Okay to Say
No and Rest"*

There's a guilt that sneaks in when you start saying no.

A whisper that questions, "Are you being selfish? Are you letting them down?"

For years, I said yes out of fear. Fear of missing out. Fear of disappointing others. Fear that if I didn't do it, no one else would.

I was stretched so thin trying to be everything for everybody that I didn't realize how much of myself I was giving away in

PART I: REFLECTION

the name of being "nice."

But God began to deal with me in the quiet:
 "**Daughter, every yes has a cost. Make sure it's one I asked you to pay.**"

Boundaries aren't walls to keep others out. They're fences that protect what God is cultivating within. Just as a garden needs a gate to grow safely, your life needs limits to flourish.

Boundaries don't mean you're less loving — they mean you're becoming more wise.

The Invitation:

This is your moment to check your yeses.

Ask the Holy Spirit to show you:

- *What have I said yes to out of obligation, not obedience?*

- *Where do I need to draw a healthy boundary to protect my peace?*

- *How would my life shift if I honored the word "no" as an act of rest?*

PART I: REFLECTION

Then practice a boundary today. It doesn't have to be loud or dramatic. It could sound like:

- "I'm not available for that today."
- "Let me get back to you after I've had time to pray."
- "I'm choosing rest in this season, so I can't take that on."

Why This Matters:

When your calendar is filled with yeses that God never required, it becomes harder to hear what He's actually calling you to do.

Rest requires room. And room requires boundaries. The same way Jesus stepped away from the crowds, you too are allowed to step back without explanation.

You don't owe everyone access to you. You only owe God your alignment.

PART I: REFLECTION

Journal Prompt:

- Where do I feel stretched thin?

- Have I been saying yes to things God never assigned to me?

- What kind of boundaries would help me rest well and serve better?

PART I: REFLECTION

🦋 What would it look like to protect my peace without guilt?

_____

_____

_____

_____

God's Promises to Carry With You:

"Let your 'Yes' be 'Yes,' and your 'No,' 'No'; anything more than this comes from the evil one." — Matthew 5:37 (NIV)

"Above all else, guard your heart, for everything you do flows from it." — Proverbs 4:23 (NIV)

Your Rest Word:

Guard

Guarding your peace is not a betrayal — it's obedience.

PART II

Environment

CREATE PEACE AROUND YOU

*Your outer space reflects your inner world.
Shift the setting to support the stillness.*

PART II: ENVIRONMENT

INVITATION 11:

Just Breathe

*"You're Not Behind,
You're Being Held"*

There's a pressure that creeps in quietly — a belief that you're always late to your own life. Like you missed the moment. Like you should've been further by now.

Doing more. Achieving more. Becoming more.

Maybe you've said things like:

"I thought I'd be married by now."
"I should have more saved up."
"I wasted too much time — I'm behind."

PART II: ENVIRONMENT

But here's the truth no one told us loud enough: **God is not in a rush. And He's not measuring you by the world's timeline.**

Just because something hasn't happened yet doesn't mean it never will. You're not delayed — you're being developed. You're not forgotten—you're being formed.

The breath of God didn't just give you life, it sustains it.

When you pause to breathe, you're not quitting. You're receiving.

There's grace in the pause. There's clarity in the quiet. And there's rest in remembering that **you're being held, not hurried.**

PART II: ENVIRONMENT

The Invitation:

Take a breath. Literally.

Place one hand on your chest and the other on your belly. Inhale slowly. Exhale slowly. Do this for 2–3 minutes. Let your body come into agreement with God's peace.

Then say out loud:

- "I am not behind."
- "I am exactly where God has me."
- "My breath is proof I'm still becoming."

This moment is not lost. It's sacred. It's a reminder that rest doesn't mean stepping back — it means *coming back* to who you really are.

PART II: ENVIRONMENT

Why This Matters:

So many people are living life on fast-forward — constantly chasing, constantly comparing. But your soul wasn't built for pressure. It was built for presence.

Every time you breathe deeply, you say no to the lie that urgency is holy. You declare that **God's timing is still trustworthy.**

That you are held — not by expectations, but by eternal hands.

Journal Prompt:

- Where in my life do I feel like I'm "behind"?

PART II: ENVIRONMENT

🦋 What pressure am I carrying that God never asked me to hold?

🦋 How can I anchor myself in divine timing instead of deadlines?

🦋 What does breathing with God — not racing ahead — look like for me right now?

PART II: ENVIRONMENT

God's Promises to Carry With You:

"The Lord is good to those who wait for Him, to the soul who seeks Him." — Lamentations 3:25 (ESV)

"He makes everything beautiful in its time." — Ecclesiastes 3:11 (NLT)

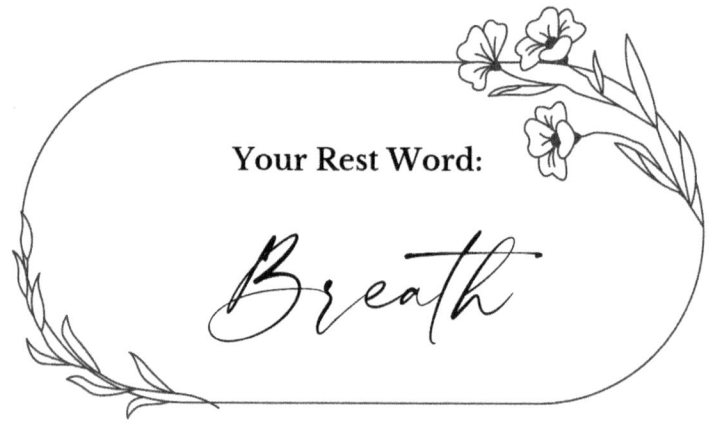

Your Rest Word: *Breath*

Every breath is a reminder:
You're not behind. You're being held.

PART II: ENVIRONMENT

INVITATION 12:

Prepare a Place for Peace

*"Your Environment
Can Minister to You"*

Have you ever walked into a space and instantly felt lighter? Or entered a room and felt tension rise — even when nothing was being said?

That's because **environments carry messages.** Some whisper calm. Others shout chaos.

Your surroundings are not just background noise — they're partners in your rhythm of rest. When your space is cluttered, noisy, or draining, it begins to shape your thoughts and emotional state more than you realize.

PART II: ENVIRONMENT

I remember when I was in a season of decision fatigue. Everything felt loud — not just the people, but the piles of mail on the counter, the clothes on the chair, the endless notifications on my phone. My physical space reflected my inner world: scattered and overstimulated.

One day, I lit a candle, turned on soft worship music, and cleared just one small area — my desk. I exhaled. Something shifted. That corner became my invitation to breathe again. Not because it was perfect — but because it was **intentional**.

The Invitation:

You don't have to do a full makeover. Simply choose one space — a corner, a desk, a nightstand — and prepare it to welcome rest. Think of it as your peace corner.

A few gentle ways to do this:

- *Clear any clutter or items that don't reflect calm.*

- *Add something that soothes your senses — a candle, a soft throw, a framed scripture.*

- *Play soft instrumental or worship music for five minutes in that space.*

PART II: ENVIRONMENT

> 🦋 *Speak a blessing over the area:*
>
> *"Let this place hold peace, not pressure."*
>
> You are not just creating order — you're creating an atmosphere that agrees with God's presence.

Why This Matters:

Your environment either partners with your rest or pulls you away from it. It can be a sanctuary or a source of subtle stress.

When you prepare space with peace in mind, you're sending a signal to your nervous system and your spirit: *It's safe to exhale here.*

And that message can carry you through even the busiest days.

Peace isn't found in perfection. It's found in presence. And presence can be prepared.

PART II: ENVIRONMENT

Journal Prompt:

🦋 What area of my home feels the most peaceful right now? Why?

_____
_____
_____
_____

🦋 What part of my environment feels chaotic or draining?

_____
_____
_____
_____

🦋 How might I refresh just one space to serve as a reset point each day?

_____
_____
_____
_____

PART II: ENVIRONMENT

🦋 What would it look like to invite God into the atmosphere of my home — room by room?

_____

_____

_____

_____

God's Promises to Carry With You:

> *"My people will live in peaceful dwelling places, in secure homes, in undisturbed places of rest."* — Isaiah 32:18 (NIV)

> *"The Lord bless you and keep you; the Lord make His face shine upon you and be gracious to you."* — Numbers 6:24-25 (NIV)

Your Rest Word: *Atmosphere*

Peace is not just a feeling — it can be something you prepare, steward, and carry into every space.

PART II: ENVIRONMENT

INVITATION 13:

Rest Doesn't Mean You're Weak

"Even Jesus Took Naps"

Somewhere along the way, rest got labeled as laziness. Pausing was seen as quitting. Naps were dismissed as indulgent. And the only time people gave themselves permission to slow down was when they hit a wall.

But pause with me for a moment: **even Jesus took naps.**

In the middle of a storm, on a boat, while chaos brewed around Him — He rested. Not because He didn't care, but because He was secure. He had nothing to prove, nothing to panic about. His confidence in the Father allowed Him to

PART II: ENVIRONMENT

sleep in peace.

You don't have to wait until you're worn out to rest. You don't have to earn rest through exhaustion. And rest is not a reward — it's a rhythm.

You are not weak when you rest. You're wise.

> ## The Invitation:
>
> Choose one way today to rest on purpose — not because you're tired, but because you're worthy of rest. Let it be a bold declaration: *Rest is holy work.*
>
> Ways to begin:
>
> - *Lie down for 20 minutes with your phone in another room.*
> - *Watch the trees move outside your window — just observe, without multitasking.*
> - *Make a cup of tea and sit in silence, savoring the warmth.*
>
> Rest can be simple. It can be still. It can be sacred — without performance.

PART II: ENVIRONMENT

Why This Matters:

When you rest intentionally, you reclaim your strength. You're no longer reacting to burnout — you're choosing a rhythm that honors your body, mind, and spirit. Even more, you're aligning yourself with the example Jesus set.

He wasn't rushed.
He wasn't overwhelmed.

And when He needed to withdraw and rest — He did.

If the Savior of the world didn't equate rest with weakness, neither should we.

Journal Prompt:

What story have I believed about rest and weakness?

_____
_____
_____
_____
_____

PART II: ENVIRONMENT

🦋 What would it look like to rest from a place of confidence, not crisis?

🦋 How might Jesus' example shift the way I view rest in my own life?

🦋 What kind of rest does my soul crave right now?

PART II: ENVIRONMENT

God's Promises to Carry With You:

"In peace I will lie down and sleep, for You alone, Lord, make me dwell in safety." — Psalm 4:8 (NIV)

"The Lord replied, 'My Presence will go with you, and I will give you rest.'" — Exodus 33:14 (NIV)

Your Rest Word: Strength

Rest isn't the absence of strength — it's where strength is renewed.

PART II: ENVIRONMENT

INVITATION 14:

Rest as Resistance

*"You Don't Have to Be
Everything to Everyone"*

There's a quiet pressure that creeps in — the one that tells you if you don't do it, no one will. That if you stop showing up for everyone else, the world might unravel. So you push through. Smile. Say yes. Make it all work.

But underneath the capable surface is a soul that's tired of carrying what was never hers to hold.

Let's be honest — there's a part of you that's afraid to rest because you think rest will make you less needed. Less valuable. Less responsible.

PART II: ENVIRONMENT

That's not truth. That's bondage.

You don't have to prove your worth through constant availability.

You don't have to stretch yourself to the edge just to feel useful.

Rest is not neglect — it's resistance. It's how you say no to performing and yes to being.

Even Jesus wasn't "everything to everyone" every moment. He set boundaries. He stepped away from the crowds. He prioritized time with the Father. And when people came with demands, sometimes... He said no.

If Jesus could rest — with the weight of the world on His shoulders — so can you.

PART II: ENVIRONMENT

The Invitation:

Today, pause and ask yourself:

Who am I over-serving to prove my value?

Then choose one boundary to honor:

🦋 *Let a call go to voicemail.*

🦋 *Say, "I'm not available today, but I can follow up tomorrow."*

🦋 *Leave one item unchecked on your to-do list and rest instead.*

These are not acts of irresponsibility — they are acts of resistance against burnout culture.

Why This Matters:

When you say yes to everything, you quietly say no to your well-being. But when you rest, you reclaim your time, your energy, and your identity as **God's — not everyone's answer.**

You don't need to be everything. You were never meant to be.

PART II: ENVIRONMENT

And sometimes, obedience sounds like:
"I need to rest right now. I trust God to hold the rest."

Journal Prompt:

- Where in my life do I feel the pressure to be "everything"?

- Who or what am I afraid of disappointing if I rest?

- What would healthy boundaries look like in this season?

PART II: ENVIRONMENT

🦋 What does God say about my worth when I'm doing less?

_____

_____

_____

_____

God's Promises to Carry With You:

> *"Am I now trying to win the approval of human beings, or of God?... If I were still trying to please people, I would not be a servant of Christ."* — Galatians 1:10 (NIV)

> *"Be still before the Lord and wait patiently for Him."* — Psalm 37:7a (NIV)

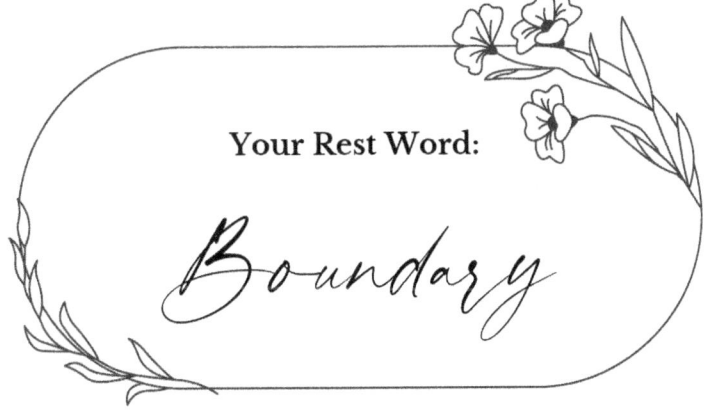

Your Rest Word: *Boundary*

Every "no" you give with grace is a door God can walk through with peace.

PART II: ENVIRONMENT

INVITATION 15:

Rest from Comparison

*"You Don't Have to
Measure Up to Be Loved"*

"There's no peace in trying to wear someone else's calling."

It starts subtly. You scroll past someone else's highlight reel and feel that quiet ache in your chest. Maybe you're not doing enough. Maybe you missed your moment. Maybe if you just tried harder, looked different, talked different... then you'd be further along.

Comparison doesn't always shout. Sometimes it whispers. It doesn't just make you feel less than — it makes you

PART II: ENVIRONMENT

question if God's plan for you is enough. I remember a season when I was measuring my life against everyone else's progress. Their milestones felt like markers of my delay. The enemy had me so distracted watching their race that I kept stumbling in my own. God interrupted those thoughts with a gentle nudge:

"Daughter, your pace is holy."

Those four words shifted everything.

You don't have to match someone else's rhythm.
You don't have to mimic their expression, their success, their anointing.

Your assignment is personal. So is your timing.

Rest means **no more chasing someone else's finish line.**

 Rest means releasing the pressure to compare and leaning into God's custom-designed purpose for you.

PART II: ENVIRONMENT

The Invitation:

Today, resist the urge to measure your life by someone else's ruler.

Choose one of these practices:

- *Mute or unfollow an account that triggers comparison.*

- *Write down 5 things God is doing in your life right now — even if they seem small.*

- *Say aloud:*
  "God, I trust the pace You've set for me."

- *Look in the mirror and thank God for your gifts, your voice, your lane.*

Let rest silence the lies that say you're behind. You are **becoming**, not competing.

PART II: ENVIRONMENT

Why This Matters:

Comparison creates soul fatigue. It clouds your vision and distracts you from the joy right in front of you.

When you rest from comparison, you return to **gratitude**.

You begin to see yourself through God's eyes again — chosen, equipped, and deeply loved.

You stop asking, "Why not me?" and start declaring, "Lord, thank You for what is mine."

Who or what do I often compare myself to — and why?

PART II: ENVIRONMENT

🦋 What has God spoken over my life that I've forgotten because I'm watching someone else?

_____
_____
_____
_____
_____

🦋 How do I feel when I focus on my lane and my pace?

_____
_____
_____
_____
_____

🦋 What's one area where I can choose to celebrate instead of compare?

_____
_____
_____
_____
_____

PART II: ENVIRONMENT

God's Promises to Carry With You:

"I praise You because I am fearfully and wonderfully made; Your works are wonderful, I know that full well."
— Psalm 139:14 (NIV)

"Each one should test their own actions. Then they can take pride in themselves alone, without comparing themselves to someone else." — Galatians 6:4 (NIV)

Your Rest Word: *Enough*

You don't need to be them.
You've already been chosen as you.

PART II: ENVIRONMENT

INVITATION 16:

Rest in God's Timing

*"You're Not Behind
— You're Being Prepared"*

Delay doesn't mean denial.

It may just mean development."

There are moments when it feels like everyone else is arriving — and you're still waiting. Waiting for the opportunity. The confirmation. The breakthrough. You've prayed. Prepared. Showed up again and again. And yet... the door hasn't opened.

In that space, doubt tries to settle in. Maybe you missed it.

PART II: ENVIRONMENT

Maybe you're behind. Maybe it's too late.

But here's the truth: **God is never rushed. And you are not late.**

You are on Heaven's timeline — not the world's.

I remember asking God why something hadn't happened yet. I had done the work. I had said yes. And still, it felt like I was sitting in pause while everyone else pressed play. His reply was quiet, but it anchored me:

"What I'm building in you is greater than what you're asking Me for."

That moment reminded me that timing is not just about what we're waiting to receive — it's about who we're becoming in the waiting.

Sometimes, rest means trusting that your *becoming* is just as important as your *arriving*.

PART II: ENVIRONMENT

The Invitation:

Pause the pressure to force what's not ready. Today, choose one small way to rest in God's timing:

- *Light a candle and breathe deeply while whispering,*
  "God, I surrender my timeline to Yours."

- *Write down what you're waiting for — then list three things you're learning in the wait.*

- *Delete one deadline that wasn't Spirit-led, just self-imposed.*

- *Thank God in advance for the doors He's preparing that you can't yet see.*

Why This Matters:

We often wear urgency like armor. We treat delay like punishment. But God sees what we cannot. He knows what we're not ready for. And He protects us in the process.

When you rest in God's timing, you're not giving up

PART II: ENVIRONMENT

— you're aligning. You're saying, "God, I trust that You know what's best and when it's best."

That trust becomes a sanctuary. A steady place to breathe while everything else moves.

Journal Prompt:

🦋 Where in my life am I feeling impatient or rushed right now?

_____
_____
_____
_____

🦋 What has God done in the past while I was waiting that I can now see clearly?

_____
_____
_____
_____

PART II: ENVIRONMENT

🦋 How might this waiting season be preparing me for something greater?

_____
_____
_____
_____
_____

🦋 What can I do this week to embrace the pace of peace?

_____
_____
_____
_____
_____

God's Promises to Carry With You:

"He has made everything beautiful in its time."
— Ecclesiastes 3:11a (NIV)

"For the vision is yet for the appointed time; it testifies about the end and will not lie. Though it delays, wait for it, since it will certainly come and not be late." — Habakkuk 2:3 (CSB)

PART II: ENVIRONMENT

Your Rest Word: Trust

Your timeline isn't broken.
It's being held by the One who sees the whole picture.

PART II: ENVIRONMENT

INVITATION 17:

Rest in the Unknown

*"You Don't Need All the Answers
to Take the Next Step"*

Faith doesn't erase the unknown. It invites you to walk through it with God.

There are seasons when clarity feels distant. When the map isn't laid out, and the road ahead is foggy. You've prayed, listened, and waited — but still, the next step feels uncertain.

You want a sign. A confirmation. Something that tells you you're not just wandering.

But sometimes God doesn't show you the whole path — just the next right step.

PART II: ENVIRONMENT

That used to frustrate me. I wanted the full picture, the complete plan, the timeline in hand. But over and over again, God would gently whisper,
"You don't need the whole plan. You just need Me."

That truth became a comfort. I didn't have to have it all figured out. I just had to stay close to the One who did.

The unknown is not a punishment — it's a place of invitation. A space where we surrender our obsession with certainty and practice trust in the present.

The Invitation:

Release the pressure to "have it all together." Today, let yourself rest without knowing all the answers:

- 🦋 *Go for a walk without a destination and simply talk to God.*

- 🦋 *Light a lamp and journal about what's unclear — then pray,*
  "God, give me peace before clarity."

- 🦋 *Write a list of things you do know — remind yourself of what's steady even in shifting times.*

PART II: ENVIRONMENT

 Speak this aloud:
"I don't have to know everything. I just have to walk with God."

Why This Matters:

We often link peace to having control. But real peace comes from knowing we are held even when we're unsure.

Resting in the unknown teaches us to depend on God's character, not just His answers.

It quiets the anxiety that says, "What if?" and replaces it with the faith that says, "Even if."

Journal Prompt:

What part of my life feels the most uncertain right now?

_____

_____

_____

_____

PART II: ENVIRONMENT

🦋 How is God inviting me to trust instead of figure everything out?

_____
_____
_____
_____

🦋 What truth can I hold on to in this in-between season?

_____
_____
_____
_____

🦋 Where have I seen God guide me before — even when I couldn't see the outcome?

_____
_____
_____
_____

PART II: ENVIRONMENT

God's Promises to Carry With You:

"Trust in the Lord with all your heart and lean not on your own understanding; in all your ways submit to Him, and He will make your paths straight."
— Proverbs 3:5–6 (NIV)

"Whether you turn to the right or to the left, your ears will hear a voice behind you, saying, 'This is the way; walk in it.'" — Isaiah 30:21 (NIV)

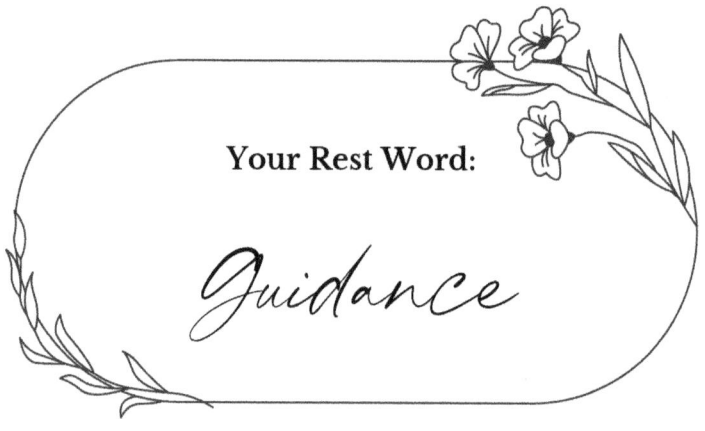

Your Rest Word:

Guidance

You may not see the whole path,
but God's voice will always light your next step.

PART II: ENVIRONMENT

INVITATION 18:

Rest in the Becoming

*"You're Still Growing,
and That's Enough"*

Becoming is a quiet process. Not always loud. Not always clear. It happens in the hidden places — in the pauses between success and failure, in the middle of what's no longer and what's not yet.

We don't always see our own growth. We notice what's unfinished before we notice what's shifting. We fixate on what hasn't bloomed, forgetting the beauty of being rooted.

You may look at your life and feel like you're behind. Like you should be further along. Doing more. Producing more.

PART II: ENVIRONMENT

Showing more results.

But God never rushed a seed to become a tree. He lets things unfold — on time, in purpose, by design.

I had to learn that, too. I used to measure progress by how much I could produce. But God was more interested in how I was being shaped. Not just what I did, but who I was becoming.

There's a version of you that God is forming — gently, intentionally. And you don't have to strive your way into it. You can rest and still grow. In fact, real growth often requires rest.

The Invitation:

Let go of the pressure to perform progress. Let yourself be in process. Try one of these gentle resets:

- *Revisit an old journal and highlight any growth you now see in hindsight.*

- *Speak these words over yourself:*
  "God, give me peace before clarity."

PART II: ENVIRONMENT

> 🦋 *Give yourself permission to leave one thing unfinished today.*
>
> 🦋 *Spend 10 quiet minutes asking God:*
> *"What are You shaping in me right now?"*

Why This Matters:

Growth is not always visible, but that doesn't make it any less real. When you rest in the becoming, you stop rushing yourself and start honoring the rhythm of grace.

God does His best work in the soil before the harvest ever shows. Trust the roots He's building in you.

🦋 Where am I placing pressure on myself to "arrive"?

_____

_____

_____

_____

PART II: ENVIRONMENT

🦋 What growth has happened in me that I've overlooked or minimized?

_____
_____
_____
_____

🦋 What is God teaching me about grace in this season of becoming?

_____
_____
_____
_____

🦋 How can I honor the pace God has chosen for me?

_____
_____
_____
_____

PART II: ENVIRONMENT

God's Promises to Carry With You:

"Being confident of this, that He who began a good work in you will carry it on to completion until the day of Christ Jesus." — Philippians 1:6 (NIV)

"Let us not become weary in doing good, for at the proper time we will reap a harvest if we do not give up."
— Galatians 6:9 (NIV)

Your Rest Word: *Becoming*

You are not behind —
you're blooming in ways heaven already sees.

PART III

Stillness

STAY PRESENT IN GOD'S PRESENCE

*Your outer space reflects your inner world.
It's not about pausing your schedule. It's about pausing your soul.*

PART III: STILLNESS

INVITATION 19:

Rest in God's Nearness

*"You're not alone in this
— not for a moment."*

*T*he Lord is close to the brokenhearted and saves those who are crushed in spirit." — Psalm 34:18 (NIV)

There's a kind of weariness that doesn't come from what you're doing — it comes from what you feel you're facing alone.

You may have smiled all day, checked every box, showed up with grace — and still felt invisible. You carry burdens no one sees. Worries you can't explain. Questions you're tired of asking.

PART III: STILLNESS

But there's One who doesn't need an explanation. God doesn't wait until you're strong again to come close. He draws near when your voice trembles. When your chest feels tight. When all you can do is exhale, "Lord, I'm tired."

His nearness is not conditional — it's constant.

Even when you're overwhelmed. Even when you're unsure. Even when your faith feels small.

Especially then.

Because presence is one of His promises.

And resting in His nearness doesn't mean your circumstances change instantly. It means you're not carrying them alone. His nearness doesn't rush you. It holds you.

You don't have to fix your face to pray. You don't have to find the perfect words. You don't even have to feel brave.

You just have to be still long enough to notice... **He's already here.**

PART III: STILLNESS

The Invitation:

Take 3 minutes to pause. Right where you are.

Let your heart whisper this prayer:

"God, I don't have all the answers. But I trust You're near. That's enough for today."

Then gently ask yourself:

🦋 *Where do I feel most alone right now?*

🦋 *Where might God already be present, though I haven't noticed?*

No need to overthink it. This is a rest stop, not a performance.

Why This Matters:

We often assume spiritual rest requires spiritual strength. But sometimes it's our weakness that welcomes Him best.

God doesn't withdraw when we're weary — He leans in.

PART III: STILLNESS

And certainly not in silence.

Resting in God's nearness reminds you:

- *You are seen.*
- *You are held.*
- *You are never abandoned.*

Journal Prompt:

- What area of my life feels the most isolated or unseen?

_____
_____
_____
_____

- When have I felt God's presence the most clearly — and what was different about that moment?

_____
_____
_____
_____

PART III: STILLNESS

🦋 How can I make space to notice God in my ordinary moments this week?

_____
_____
_____
_____
_____

🦋 What would it mean to truly believe, "God is close to me right now"?

_____
_____
_____
_____
_____

God's Promises to Carry With You:

> *"Never will I leave you; never will I forsake you."*
> — Hebrews 13:5b (NIV)

> *"Even when I walk through the darkest valley, I will not be afraid, for You are close beside me."* — Psalm 23:4a (NLT)

PART III: STILLNESS

Your Rest Word: *Presence*

You don't have to chase what's already with you.
God is here.

PART III: STILLNESS

INVITATION 20:

Rest from Performance —
"You're Not God's Project"

"You don't have to perform for
love. You already have it."

*T*here's a pressure that doesn't always come from the outside
— it lives in the quiet thoughts that say, "I should be further along."
"I should have it together by now."
"I should be more spiritual, more productive, more consistent."

We say we trust God — but sometimes we treat our lives like a never-ending to-do list. We think if we can just perform a little better, God will be more pleased. But the truth is, God isn't grading you. He's guiding you.

You're not a project to be fixed.

PART III: STILLNESS

You're a person to be loved.

Rest is the brave choice to stop striving for approval you already have. It's the holy release of performance in exchange for presence. When you let go of what you think proves your worth, you make room to receive the worth God already gave.

Even Jesus didn't hustle to prove His identity. Before He ever preached a sermon, healed a soul, or went to the cross, the Father said:

"This is my beloved Son, in whom I am well pleased." — **Matthew 3:17 (KJV)**

Before the performance, there was love.
And that's your story too.

PART III: STILLNESS

The Invitation:

Take a moment to sit with this truth: You are deeply loved, before you do anything else.
Then, ask yourself:

- 🦋 *What am I doing right now to prove something God has already spoken?*

- 🦋 *Where am I confusing productivity with purpose?*

- 🦋 *How might God be inviting me to simply be?*

Let today be a break from performance. Not because you're giving up — but because you're finally letting God lead.

Why This Matters:

When your worth is tied to what you do, rest will always feel risky. But when your identity is rooted in who God says you are, rest becomes a response — not a reward.

You were never created to impress your way into peace. You were created to live from peace — and let God finish what He started.

PART III: STILLNESS

Journal Prompt:

- What do I feel I have to "earn" right now — love, validation, rest, success?

- Where did I learn that doing more made me more valuable?

- What would my schedule look like if I truly believed I was enough as I am?

PART III: STILLNESS

God's Promises to Carry With You:

"It is finished." — John 19:30 (KJV)

"Being confident of this very thing, that he which hath begun a good work in you will perform it until the day of Jesus Christ." — Philippians 1:6 (KJV)

Your Rest Word:

Hope

PART III: STILLNESS

INVITATION 21:

Rest From Regret

*"God's mercy goes further than
your missteps."*

*F*orget the former things; do not dwell on the past. See, I am doing a new thing!" — Isaiah 43:18–19 (NIV)

There are memories you'd rather not revisit.
Moments you wish you could edit.
Words you'd take back.
Decisions you would unmake in a heartbeat.

Regret has a way of replaying old footage in your mind, always highlighting what you *should've* done, where you *could've* been, and who you *might've* become.

PART III: STILLNESS

It whispers, "You blew it," and then pretends that grace doesn't apply to people like you.

But that's not what God says.

God says He redeems. He restores. He remembers your sins no more.

Resting from regret isn't about pretending the past didn't happen. It's about choosing not to live there.

There is more ahead than there is behind you.
There is more grace than there was failure.

And the God who knew every misstep before you made it still chose to call you His own.

PART III: STILLNESS

The Invitation:

Today, bring one moment of regret before God. Write it down — not to dwell on it, but to release it.

Then declare aloud:

"I don't live there anymore. I am forgiven, I am free, and I am moving forward."

This is your sacred permission to let the past stay in the past.

Why This Matters:

When regret takes root, it stunts your growth. You hesitate. You question yourself. You forfeit opportunities out of guilt instead of walking in the freedom Christ already purchased.

But rest is a declaration that your identity is not in what you've done — it's in who God says you are now.

He specializes in turning broken roads into divine highways.

PART III: STILLNESS

Journal Prompt:

- What regret am I still holding on to that God has already forgiven?

- How have I allowed shame to shape my decisions?

- What does freedom from that regret actually look like in my daily life?

PART III: STILLNESS

🦋 How can I remind myself of God's mercy when old memories resurface?

God's Promises to Carry With You:

"Therefore, if anyone is in Christ, the new creation has come: The old has gone, the new is here!"
— 2 Corinthians 5:17 (NIV)

"As far as the east is from the west, so far has He removed our transgressions from us." — Psalm 103:12 (NIV)

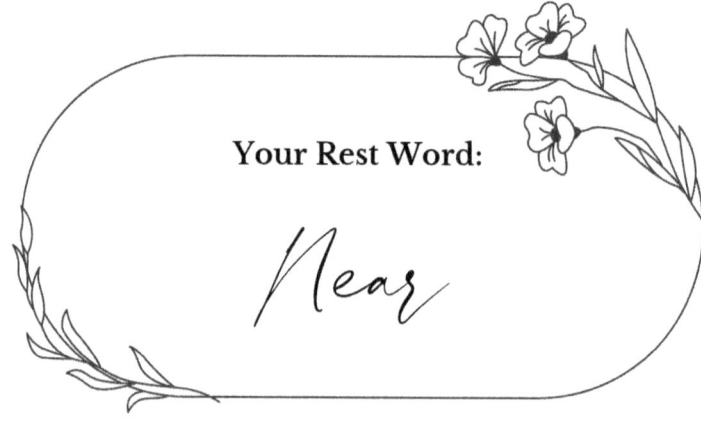

Your Rest Word: Near

PART III: STILLNESS

INVITATION 22:

Rest From External Pressure

*"God's approval carries more
weight than their expectations."*

"*F*ear of man will prove to be a snare, but whoever trusts in the Lord is kept safe." — Proverbs 29:25 (NIV)

There's a pressure that doesn't always come from within — it comes from the outside.
From what people think you *should* do.
From who they think you *should* be.
From roles and responsibilities that feel more assigned than accepted.

It's the quiet weight of expectations.

PART III: STILLNESS

Sometimes spoken. Often assumed.

It piles on until your own voice feels buried under everyone else's.

But God didn't call you to live bound by pressure. He called you to live led by peace.

External pressure is loud — but His presence is louder when we pause to listen.

There will always be people with opinions.
There will always be voices telling you to do more, be more, prove more.

But the still, small voice of the Father says:
"You are enough in Me. You don't have to perform to be protected."

PART III: STILLNESS

The Invitation:

Today, take one expectation, whether real or perceived, and lay it at God's feet.

You might write it out:

"They expect me to always be available."
"They expect me to never say no."

Then pray,

"God, help me release this weight and remember that what You ask of me is never heavy."

Give yourself room to just be, not perform.

Why This Matters:

External pressure wears down your joy and drowns out your discernment. When you're always living for others' approval, you lose sight of God's direction.

But when you rest, you remember that God never asked you to be perfect — just present.
   And that's enough.

PART III: STILLNESS

Journal Prompt:

🦋 What expectation has been weighing on me the most lately?

🦋 Who am I afraid of disappointing — and why?

🦋 What truth does God speak over my life that contradicts this pressure?

PART III: STILLNESS

🦋 How can I choose peace over performance this week?

_____

_____

_____

God's Promises to Carry With You:

"The Lord gives strength to His people; the Lord blesses His people with peace." — Psalm 29:11 (NIV)

"It is for freedom that Christ has set us free. Stand firm, then, and do not let yourselves be burdened again by a yoke of slavery." — Galatians 5:1 (NIV)

Your Rest Word:

Peace

Their opinions may shift, but God's peace is steady.

PART III: STILLNESS

INVITATION 23:

Rest in the Middle

*"When the Answer
Hasn't Come Yet"*

"Wait for the Lord; be strong and take heart and wait for the Lord." — Psalm 27:14 (NIV)

There's a place in the journey that doesn't get enough attention:

The middle.
You're not where you were.
You're not yet where you're going.
You're in between — praying, waiting, trusting... and wondering.

PART III: STILLNESS

The middle is tender. It tests your patience, your perspective, and your peace.

It's where clarity feels delayed, and answers don't always arrive when you expect them to.

And yet, **God meets us there — not just at the destination.**

You may not know when the breakthrough is coming.
You may not see how the pieces will come together.
But rest reminds you that delay is not denial — and that silence is not absence.

God is still working... even in the quiet.

PART III: STILLNESS

The Invitation:

Take five minutes today and sit with this phrase:

"I may not have the answer, but I'm still held."

You might say it aloud.
You might write it slowly across a page.
You might place your hand on your heart and simply breathe.

This isn't about forcing faith.
It's about giving yourself permission to rest in the truth that God is present — even in the pause.

Why This Matters:

Resting in the middle teaches you to trust what you can't trace.

It invites you to stop searching for signs and start settling into God's steady love.

Waiting doesn't mean nothing is happening.

It means God is preparing you for what is next — and protecting you from what isn't ready yet.

PART III: STILLNESS

Journal Prompt:

🦋 What am I waiting on that's making me feel unsettled?

🦋 How can I remind myself that God is near, even without answers?

🦋 What would it look like to rest well while I wait?

PART III: STILLNESS

🦋 When has God shown up before — even after a long silence?

_____

_____

_____

_____

God's Promises to Carry With You:

"The Lord is good to those whose hope is in Him, to the one who seeks Him." — Lamentations 3:25 (NIV)

"In quietness and trust is your strength." — Isaiah 30:15b (NIV)

Your Rest Word: *Approved*

PART III: STILLNESS

INVITATION 24:

Rest from People-Pleasing

*"You Can Be Kind and
Still Have Boundaries"*

"*Fear of man will prove to be a snare, but whoever trusts in the Lord is kept safe.*" — Proverbs 29:25 (NIV)

There's a tension many of us know too well — the weight of trying to please everyone.

You say yes when you mean maybe.

You overextend, over-apologize, over-explain.
Not out of obligation... but out of fear , fear of being misunderstood, rejected, or seen as selfish.

PART III: STILLNESS

Somewhere along the way, kindness became confused with over-commitment.

But here's the truth:
You are allowed to say no without guilt.
You are allowed to disappoint someone and still be walking in love.

And you are allowed to rest — not just physically, but emotionally — from the exhausting chase of approval.

Jesus didn't bend Himself to fit everyone's preferences.

He moved with intention, spoke with clarity, and withdrew without explanation.

You can be kind.
You can be gracious.
And you can still have boundaries.

PART III: STILLNESS

The Invitation:

Today, give yourself space to rest from needing to be understood or liked by everyone.

Try one of the following:

- *Write down a recurring situation where you say yes out of pressure — then rewrite what a healthy boundary would sound like.*

- *Practice saying,*
  "I appreciate you thinking of me, but I can't commit to that right now."

- *Remind yourself that peace is more important than performance.*

Let your spirit rest from performance-based acceptance. You are already accepted by God.

PART III: STILLNESS

Why This Matters:

The pressure to please keeps your soul in a cycle of depletion.

You start living for others' comfort instead of from God's confidence.

But when you step out of that cycle, you step into deeper peace — a peace that doesn't require constant validation.

Boundaries don't make you distant.

They make you whole.

Journal Prompt:

Where am I overextending to earn someone's approval?

_____
_____
_____
_____

PART III: STILLNESS

🦋 What fear drives my people-pleasing?

🦋 What would it look like to prioritize peace over performance?

🦋 How is God inviting me to redefine what it means to be loving?

PART III: STILLNESS

God's Promises to Carry With You:

"The Lord gives strength to His people; the Lord blesses His people with peace." — Psalm 29:11 (NIV)

"So we say with confidence, 'The Lord is my helper; I will not be afraid. What can mere mortals do to me?'"
— Hebrews 13:6 (NIV)

Your Rest Word:

Redeemed

You don't have to prove yourself.
God already said you're His.

PART III: STILLNESS

INVITATION 25:

Rest When You Feel Behind

"God Is Not Rushing You"

"There is a time for everything, and a season for every activity under the heavens." — Ecclesiastes 3:1 (NIV)

You glance at the calendar and feel it again — the pressure. It's that quiet thought that says, "You should be further along by now."

You see the milestones others are hitting. The progress. The momentum.

And you wonder if you've missed something...

PART III: STILLNESS

or worse — if God has passed you by.

But let's tell the truth.

You're not behind.
You're not late.
And you're not forgotten.

The pace of your purpose is not determined by trends, timelines, or comparison.

God doesn't rush masterpieces — and He's not rushing you.

Sometimes the greatest progress happens in stillness.

While it looks like nothing is moving, heaven is aligning.

While you're waiting, **God is working**.

PART III: STILLNESS

The Invitation:

Today, rest from the urgency to catch up.

Instead of rushing to do more, slow down and ask:

- *What season am I actually in — preparation, planting, pruning, or harvest?*

- *Am I measuring my life by God's direction or man's deadlines?*

Choose one way to honor your current pace:

- *Take a break from checking timelines (social media, milestones, metrics).*

- *Reflect on one area where you've seen quiet growth this year.*

- *Whisper,*

  "God, I trust Your timing more than mine."

PART III: STILLNESS

Why This Matters:

Feeling behind creates unnecessary pressure.
It steals your peace, clouds your decisions, and makes you question your worth.

But rest reminds you that divine timing is never in a hurry — and it's never late.
God's plan is still unfolding, even in your pause

Journal Prompt:

- Where do I feel like I'm falling behind — and who told me I should be ahead?

_____
_____
_____

- What have I accomplished that I haven't taken time to celebrate?

_____
_____
_____

PART III: STILLNESS

🦋 How can I realign with God's rhythm instead of cultural pressure?

_____
_____
_____
_____
_____

🦋 What fruit is growing in me while I wait?

_____
_____
_____
_____

God's Promises to Carry With You:

"The Lord will work out His plans for my life — for Your faithful love, O Lord, endures forever."
— Psalm 138:8 (NLT)

"I am the Lord; in its time I will do this swiftly."
— Isaiah 60:22b (NIV)

PART III: STILLNESS

Your Rest Word:

Patience

When you rest in patience,
you align with God's perfect pace.

PART III: STILLNESS

INVITATION 26:

Rest When You're Discouraged

"Pause Before You Quit"

"Let us not grow weary in doing good, for at the proper time we will reap a harvest if we do not give up." — Galatians 6:9 (NIV)

Some days, the weight of doing good feels like too much.
You've been faithful. You've poured out. You've kept going.
But lately... your "yes" feels heavy. The reward feels far. The results feel invisible.

You're not trying to walk away forever.
You just want a break from the pressure, the pushing, the pouring.

PART III: STILLNESS

You want to feel like your effort matters. Like *you* matter.

Let me gently say this:
Your weariness is not weakness.
Your pause is not failure.

And your discouragement does not mean it's time to quit — it means **it's time to rest.**

Even Jesus paused.

When the crowds pressed in, He stepped away to breathe, to pray, to receive.
Before every major moment in His life, He made space for rest.
Not because He was giving up — but because He was refilling.

So before you make a permanent decision in a temporary moment, let **God refill what's been poured out.**

PART III: STILLNESS

The Invitation:

Today, give yourself permission to pause without shame.

Before you consider quitting, consider resting.

Try one of these:

- *Write a letter to God about what's discouraging you — no filter.*

- *List 3 small wins from the last 30 days — no matter how minor.*

- *Do something that brings joy without obligation (music, walking, laughing, journaling, praying with no agenda).*

You don't have to finish strong every day. Some days, finishing means sitting still and letting God hold you.

PART III: STILLNESS

Why This Matters:

Discouragement clouds vision. It makes you forget the seeds you've planted and the promises still unfolding.

Rest clears the fog. It helps you see the journey, not just the struggle.

It reminds you that faithfulness isn't about constant momentum — it's about staying connected.

Journal Prompt:

🦋 What's felt heavy lately — and why?

_____
_____
_____
_____

🦋 Have I been equating rest with failure?

_____
_____
_____
_____

PART III: STILLNESS

🦋 What would I say to a friend in my position right now?

_____
_____
_____
_____
_____

🦋 What does my soul need more than a solution?

_____
_____
_____
_____
_____

God's Promises to Carry With You:

"The Lord is close to the brokenhearted and saves those who are crushed in spirit." — Psalm 34:18 (NIV)

"He gives strength to the weary and increases the power of the weak." — Isaiah 40:29 (NIV)

PART III: STILLNESS

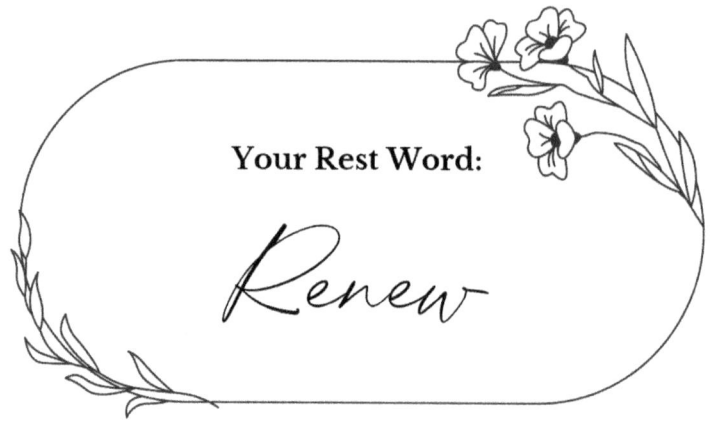

Your Rest Word: Renew

Let God renew what discouragement tried to drain.

PART III: STILLNESS

INVITATION 27:

Rest from the Need to Know Everything

*"Peace Doesn't Require
All the Answers"*

"*Trust in the Lord with all your heart and lean not on your own understanding.*" — Proverbs 3:5 (NIV)

There's a quiet exhaustion that comes from always needing to figure things out.

You rehearse the possibilities. Analyze the outcomes. Try to prepare for every "what if."
You call it planning, wisdom, responsibility. But deep down, it's fear wrapped in strategy.

PART III: STILLNESS

What if the real invitation is to release instead of *resolve*?

God never asked us to understand it all — only to trust. And trust begins where control ends.

Sometimes, peace is not found in getting an answer. It's found in surrendering the need for one.

The Invitation:

Give your mind a break from over-explaining.

Let today be a *pause from overthinking*.

Try one of these:

- 🦋 *Whisper:*

    "God, I don't need to understand. I just need to rest in You."

- 🦋 *Write out your top three "I don't know..." statements — then write "And I trust You anyway" underneath.*

- 🦋 *Take a walk without trying to solve anything — let the quiet hold your questions.*

PART III: STILLNESS

Why This Matters:

Our culture rewards certainty, but God honors trust. Trying to know everything is exhausting.

Rest is the space where you learn how to live with the questions — and still walk in peace.
When you release the pressure to "figure it all out," you make room for faith to rise.

Journal Prompt:

🦋 Where am I trying to force clarity instead of trusting God's timing?

_____
_____
_____
_____

🦋 What would it look like to rest without knowing the full picture?

_____
_____
_____

PART III: STILLNESS

🦋 What is God still trustworthy for, even when I don't have all the answers?

_____
_____
_____
_____
_____

🦋 What would peace feel like if I stopped trying to control the outcome?

_____
_____
_____
_____
_____

God's Promises to Carry With You:

"You will keep in perfect peace those whose minds are steadfast, because they trust in You." — Isaiah 26:3 (NIV)

"For we live by faith, not by sight."
— 2 Corinthians 5:7 (NIV)

PART III: STILLNESS

Your Rest Word:

Planted

PART III: STILLNESS

INVITATION 28:
Rest When You Feel Invisible

"God Still Sees You"

"Y*ou are the God who sees me."* — Genesis 16:13 (NIV)

There are moments — quiet, aching moments — when it feels like no one notices what you're carrying.

You show up, pour out, give your best... and still feel unseen.

Overlooked in rooms you prayed to be in. Forgotten by people you've been faithful to. Left out when all you did was show up with a full heart.

PART III: STILLNESS

This kind of loneliness is subtle. You might not say it out loud, but it sits in your chest like silence after applause that never came.

But here's the truth: *God sees every unseen moment.*

Every seed sown in secret. Every "yes" no one clapped for. Every tear you wiped away before anyone noticed it fell.

The One who knit you together in your mother's womb has never missed a moment of your story.

And He says — **"I see you. You matter. You are not invisible to Me."**

PART III: STILLNESS

The Invitation:

Let this be a moment to rest in being seen by God, even if you feel invisible to others.

- *Light a candle and say aloud:*

  "God, thank You for seeing me — even here."

- *Write a letter to yourself from God's perspective, reminding you of your worth.*

- *Reflect on one moment this week where you felt unseen — and invite God into that memory.*

Why This Matters:

Feeling invisible can make you shrink — questioning your value and voice.
But rest reminds you: you don't need outside validation to confirm your worth.
 Your significance isn't tied to applause — it's rooted in God's unshakable love.

Rest is how you resist the pressure to prove your worth and instead receive it.

PART III: STILLNESS

Journal Prompt:

- Where in my life do I feel unnoticed or overlooked?

- How might God be affirming me quietly in this season?

- What would it mean to rest in being fully known and fully loved?

PART III: STILLNESS

🦋 What truths do I need to remember about my value in God's eyes?

_____
_____
_____
_____

God's Promises to Carry With You:

"The Lord your God is with you, the Mighty Warrior who saves. He will take great delight in you... He will rejoice over you with singing." — Zephaniah 3:17 (NIV)

"Can a mother forget the baby at her breast...? Though she may forget, I will not forget you!" — Isaiah 49:15 (NIV)

Your Rest Word: *Seen*

You are fully known and fully seen — even in silence.

PART III: STILLNESS

INVITATION 29: Rest from Constant Productivity

"You Are Not a Machine"

In repentance and rest is your salvation, in quietness and trust is your strength." — Isaiah 30:15 (NIV)

The world will tell you that your worth is measured in output. That if you're not producing, you're not progressing. That rest is a reward — only earned after exhaustion.

But God didn't design you as a machine.

You are not built to operate without pause, without presence, without peace.

PART III: STILLNESS

Even in Eden — before sin, before shame — **rest was sacred.**

God worked six days and chose to rest on the seventh. Not because He needed it, but because we would.

He was showing us the rhythm of Heaven:
Work from rest, not just for it.

When you constantly chase productivity, you lose sight of your purpose.

You forget you're already enough — even when your hands are still.

PART III: STILLNESS

The Invitation:

Give yourself permission to rest *without guilt.*

- *Choose one task today to leave unfinished — and be okay with it.*

- *Take a nap, a walk, or sit outside without doing a thing.*

- *Say aloud:*

  "I am worthy, even when I'm not working."

This is your holy permission slip:
You don't have to earn rest — you were created for it.

Why This Matters:

When your value is tied to what you produce, you begin to treat rest like a waste. But rest is not laziness — it's obedience. It's a declaration that God is in control, not your to-do list.

Rest says:
"I trust God enough to stop striving."

PART III: STILLNESS

And in that stillness... clarity comes. Healing happens. Identity is restored.

Journal Prompt:

🦋 What lies have I believed about rest and productivity?

_____
_____
_____
_____

🦋 Where am I overworking to feel worthy?

_____
_____
_____
_____

🦋 How has God provided for me even when I did less?

_____
_____
_____
_____

PART III: STILLNESS

🦋 What would it feel like to rest before I'm exhausted?

_____

_____

_____

God's Promises to Carry With You:

"It is useless for you to work so hard from early morning until late at night... for God gives rest to His loved ones." — Psalm 127:2 (NLT)

"Come with Me by yourselves to a quiet place and get some rest." — Mark 6:31b (NIV)

Your Rest Word: *Ready*

PART III: STILLNESS

INVITATION 30:
Rest When You've Lost Your Way

*"God Knows
How to Lead You Back"*

"The Lord is my Shepherd; I shall not want. He makes me lie down in green pastures. He leads me beside still waters. He restores my soul." — Psalm 23:1–3a (ESV)

There are moments when life feels off-course.

You're doing all the right things — praying, showing up, trying your best — but somehow you still feel... lost.

Not lost in the physical sense, but in your spirit.

PART III: STILLNESS

Disoriented. Disconnected. Distant.

You wonder:

- "Have I missed something?"

- "Why does this season feel so confusing?"

- "Did I take a wrong turn?"

Let this comfort you:

God doesn't abandon you when you lose your way.
He doesn't scold you for wandering.
He meets you where you are — even in the fog.
And gently... lovingly... leads you home.

Sometimes, the only way to find yourself again is to stop searching so hard and rest in His presence.

PART III: STILLNESS

The Invitation:

Lay down your need for immediate answers.

Let today be a day of spiritual stillness.

Try one of these gentle resets:

- *Read Psalm 23 out loud — slowly. Let it breathe over your heart.*

- *Take a walk and ask, "Lord, lead me. I'm listening."*

- *Write a letter to God starting with: "Here's where I feel lost..."*

This isn't about fixing it all.

It's about finding stillness so God can *do the guiding.*

PART III: STILLNESS

Why This Matters:

When we feel lost, we often default to doing more — but clarity rarely comes from chaos.

It comes from resting in the One who knows the way — even when we don't.

God doesn't need you to map your own rescue.
He just needs you to pause long enough to receive it.

Journal Prompt:

🦋 In what area of my life do I feel spiritually off-course?

_____
_____
_____
_____

🦋 What would it look like to rest while God redirects me?

_____
_____
_____

PART III: STILLNESS

🦋 When have I experienced His guidance in the past?

_____
_____
_____
_____
_____

🦋 What is He gently inviting me to release?

_____
_____
_____
_____
_____

God's Promises to Carry With You:

> *"Whether you turn to the right or to the left, your ears will hear a voice behind you, saying, 'This is the way; walk in it.'"* — Isaiah 30:21 (NIV)

> *"I will instruct you and teach you in the way you should go; I will counsel you with my loving eye on you."*
> — Psalm 32:8 (NIV)

PART III: STILLNESS

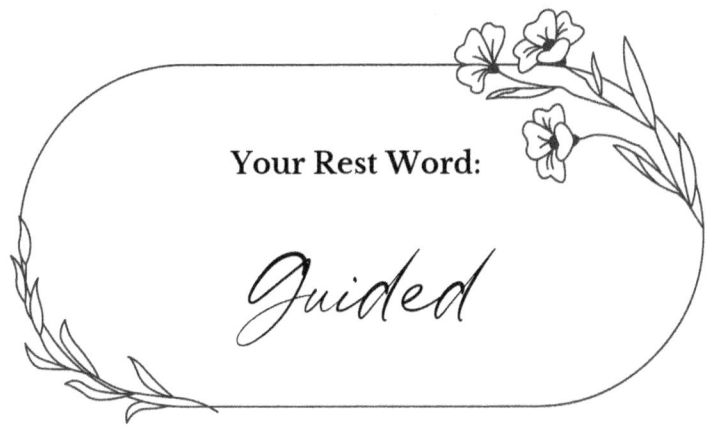

Your Rest Word:

Guided

Even when you're unsure, God is still guiding.

PART IV

Time

GIVE GOD THE FIRST AND THE REST
When you slow your pace, you hear His instructions clearly.

PART IV: TIME

INVITATION 31:
Rest in the Pause Between Seasons

*"You're Not Stuck.
You're Being Prepared*

"For everything there is a season, and a time for every matter under heaven." — Ecclesiastes 3:1 (ESV)

Some seasons are full of movement — doors opening, prayers answered, progress visible.

But then there are the in-between moments...

When one chapter has closed, but the next hasn't revealed itself yet.

PART IV: TIME

The waiting room. The hallway. The pause.

You're not where you were — but not yet where you're going.

And that space can feel uncomfortable, even discouraging.

But hear this:
This pause is not a punishment.
It's preparation.

God is not delaying your life — He's developing your roots.

PART IV: TIME

The Invitation:

Let yourself rest in the in-between without rushing clarity.

Try one or more of the following:

- 🌸 *Sit in quiet and simply say: "Lord, prepare me for what's next."*

- 🌸 *Reflect on the past season and write down what you've learned.*

- 🌸 *Light a candle and pray, "I won't force what's not ready. I will wait with You."*

Rest doesn't mean you've lost momentum.

It means you trust God's pace more than your pressure.

PART IV: TIME

Why This Matters:

We often resist the in-between because it feels uncertain.
But these pauses hold sacred preparation — where God fortifies your strength, aligns your steps, and reminds you that your value isn't based on constant movement.

God often does His deepest work in the quiet.

Journal Prompt:

🦋 What season is ending for me right now?

_____
_____
_____
_____

🦋 What do I feel God is preparing me for?

_____
_____
_____
_____

PART IV: TIME

🦋 How can I rest instead of rushing clarity?

_____
_____
_____
_____
_____

🦋 What fears or frustrations do I need to release during this pause?

_____
_____
_____
_____
_____

God's Promises to Carry With You:

> "The Lord will fulfill His purpose for me; Your steadfast love, O Lord, endures forever." — Psalm 138:8a (ESV)

> "Being confident of this, that He who began a good work in you will carry it on to completion..." — Philippians 1:6a (NIV)

PART IV: TIME

Your Rest Word:

Prepare

The pause is holy ground.
Let God work while you rest.

PART IV: TIME

INVITATION 32:

Rest from False Urgency

*"Everything That's
Pressing You Isn't From God."*

Be *still before the Lord and wait patiently for Him..."*
— *Psalm 37:7a (NIV)*

There's a voice in today's world that says *now* is the only acceptable timeline.

Reply now. Decide now. Show up now. Fix it now.

But urgency isn't always holy. And not every fire is yours to put out.

PART IV: TIME

The pressure to move quickly often masks a deeper fear:
— *If I don't act fast, I'll miss my opportunity.*
— *If I pause, they'll think I'm not committed.*
— *If I slow down, I'll fall behind.*

But what if urgency is sometimes just noise dressed as importance?

God never rushes. He leads.

And when He leads, it's never with panic — but peace.

PART IV: TIME

The Invitation:

Take a moment to separate pressure from purpose.

Ask yourself:

- *Is this God-timed or fear-driven?*
- *What would happen if I responded in peace instead of panic?*
- *Where in my day am I rushing unnecessarily?*

Then practice holy slowing:

- *Pause before answering that email or text.*
- *Take three deep breaths before making a decision.*
- *Replace "ASAP" with "As I'm led."*

PART IV: TIME

Why This Matters:

Urgency is one of the enemy's most subtle tactics. It pushes you out of alignment and into anxiety. But God doesn't need you to rush to be effective.
 He wants you to walk in rhythm — not race against fear.

Peace is your signal.
If it's not peaceful, it might not be your assignment.

Journal Prompt:

- What feels urgent right now that may not actually be important?

- Where have I felt pressure to move faster than I feel led?

PART IV: TIME

🦋 What would it look like to trust God's pace in this situation?

_____

_____

_____

_____

🦋 How can I practice "holy slowing" today?

_____

_____

_____

_____

God's Promises to Carry With You:

> *"In repentance and rest is your salvation, in quietness and trust is your strength."* — Isaiah 30:15b (NIV)

> *"The steps of a good man are ordered by the Lord."* — Psalm 37:23 (KJV)

PART IV: TIME

Your Rest Word:

Pause

Every pause is a chance to
trade pressure for peace.

PART IV: TIME

INVITATION 33:

Rest from Hustle Culture

*"You Are Not Measured by
How Much You Produce."*

He makes me lie down in green pastures..."
— Psalm 23:2a (NIV)

There's a lie that says your worth is tied to how busy you are.

That if you're not working, producing, pushing — you're falling behind.

That rest is earned only after you've given your all. And sometimes even then, it still doesn't feel like enough.

PART IV: TIME

But here's the truth:
God didn't design you for nonstop output.
You're not a machine. You're a masterpiece.
You're allowed to pause. You're allowed to stop. You're allowed to simply be.

In God's economy, rest isn't a reward — it's a rhythm.

The world claps for hustle.
But heaven calls for holiness.

And sometimes, that holiness looks like choosing rest even when no one else understands why.

PART IV: TIME

The Invitation:

Today, resist the need to "earn" your rest.

Try one of these sacred pauses:

- *Take a walk with no podcast, no goal — just you and God.*
- *Give yourself permission to nap without guilt.*
- *Block time on your calendar labeled "Stillness."*

Write this somewhere visible today:

"My worth is not up for debate — even when I'm resting."

Why This Matters:

Hustle culture will have you chasing affirmation that God already gave.

It will burn you out and call it ambition.
But God invites you to a life that's full — not frantic.
Jesus took naps on boats in the middle of storms.
You can rest, even in a season of building.

PART IV: TIME

Productivity without presence is just motion.

But rest makes space for God to move in ways hustle never can.

Journal Prompt:

🦋 What makes me feel like I have to "earn" rest?

_____
_____
_____
_____
_____

🦋 When was the last time I felt joy in just being still?

_____
_____
_____
_____
_____
_____

PART IV: TIME

🦋 What parts of hustle culture have crept into my daily mindset?

_____

_____

_____

_____

🦋 What would happen if I did less — but with God's blessing?

_____

_____

_____

_____

God's Promises to Carry With You:

"It is useless for you to work so hard from early morning until late at night... for God gives rest to His loved ones."
— Psalm 127:2 (NLT)

"My presence will go with you, and I will give you rest."
— Exodus 33:14 (NIV)

PART IV: TIME

Your Rest Word:

Safe

You are already enough — without the grind.

PART IV: TIME

INVITATION 34:

Rest in God's Presence

*"He's Closer Than
Your Next Breath."*

B e still, and know that I am God." — Psalm 46:10 (NIV)

Some days we feel as if God is somewhere far off—hidden behind busyness, distance, or disappointment. We assume we need perfect conditions, the right music, or a quiet retreat to sense Him. Yet Scripture reminds us God's presence is not an appointment we schedule; it's the atmosphere in which we live and move and have our being.

I learned this on a hectic afternoon, when every plan unraveled. Emails piled up, calls went unanswered, and my

PART IV: TIME

mind raced. In the middle of the swirl, I paused—just for a moment—and whispered, *"God, where are You?"*

A gentle thought rose in my heart: **"Right here. I never left."**

Nothing around me changed, but everything within me did. Tension loosened, peace returned, and I remembered: awareness of His presence is often one quiet breath away.

You don't have to strive for what's already with you.

Rest is not found by reaching farther; it's found by settling deeper into the truth that **God is here, now—regardless of circumstance, setting, or feeling.**

PART IV: TIME

The Invitation:

Choose five unhurried minutes today to lean into God's nearness.

- *Sit comfortably and let your shoulders drop.*

- *Inhale slowly, praying, "You are here."*

- *Exhale slowly, praying, "I am Yours."*

- *Read Psalm 46:10 once; then close your eyes and listen.*

- *Notice any gentle impressions, memories, or scriptures that surface. There's no need to force content—simply rest in awareness.*

Carry this practice into ordinary moments: standing in a checkout line, driving, folding laundry.

Every breath can become a reminder:

God with me, God in me, God for me.

PART IV: TIME

Why This Matters:

When we forget God's nearness, anxiety fills the gap. But awareness of His presence quiets striving and anchors the soul. You no longer chase peace—you receive it.

Work becomes worship, waiting becomes trust, and even weariness becomes a doorway to communion.

Journal Prompt:

- When have I most clearly sensed God's presence—and what made me aware of it?

- Where do I tend to search for God outside myself instead of within the moment?

PART IV: TIME

🦋 How might practicing simple breath-prayers shift my day?

_____
_____
_____
_____
_____

🦋 What distractions most often pull me out of awareness—and how can I gently refocus?

_____
_____
_____
_____
_____

God's Promises to Carry With You:

"The Lord your God will be with you wherever you go."
— Joshua 1:9 (NIV)

"Surely I am with you always, to the very end of the age."
— Matthew 28:20 (NIV)

PART IV: TIME

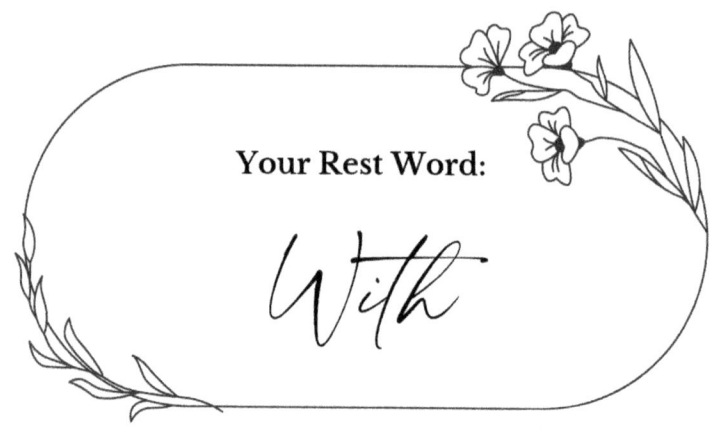

Your Rest Word:

With

Wherever you are, God is already with you
—rest in that closeness.

PART IV: TIME

INVITATION 35:

Rest from Self-Criticism

*"Grace Speaks Louder Than
Your Inner Judge"*

"There is now no condemnation for those who are in Christ Jesus." — Romans 8:1 (NIV)

Sometimes the harshest voice you hear... is your own.
That inner critic? It doesn't just whisper — it echoes.

"You should've known better."
"You always mess it up."
"You're not as disciplined, gifted, or spiritual as they are."

Those thoughts don't come from God. They don't convict —

PART IV: TIME

they accuse. And accusation will always rob rest.

Rest from self-criticism begins when we believe what God says is louder than what we feel.

God doesn't measure us by perfection — He invites us to grow through grace. He's not waiting for us to perform. He's already called us accepted, beloved, and chosen.

If we're going to rest in that truth, we must stop rehearsing shame and start repeating what grace declares:

I am not the voice of my failure. I am the fruit of God's mercy.

PART IV: TIME

The Invitation:

Practice this moment of inner rest today:

- *Write down three criticisms you've repeated to yourself lately.*

- *Cross them out one by one.*

- *Next to each one, write a truth God has spoken over you instead.*
  (Examples: "I'm behind" becomes "I am on time for my own journey.")

Then, say this aloud:

"I release the weight of my own judgment. I choose grace instead."

Why This Matters:

Self-criticism is exhausting because it keeps you in a constant courtroom. But when you remember Jesus already paid the price and took the verdict, the gavel is down.

You're free to rest in who you are becoming — not bound to who you were.

PART IV: TIME

Journal Prompt:

- What's one area where I've been overly critical of myself lately?

- Where might that inner criticism be rooted — fear, comparison, perfectionism?

- What would it sound like to speak to myself the way God speaks to me?

PART IV: TIME

🦋 How can I replace self-judgment with compassion this week?

_____

_____

_____

_____

God's Promises to Carry With You:

"The Lord is compassionate and gracious, slow to anger, abounding in love." — Psalm 103:8 (NIV)

"He has removed our sins as far from us as the east is from the west." — Psalm 103:12 (NLT)

Your Rest Word: *Mercy*

Rest doesn't wait for perfection.
Mercy meets you in your mess and still calls you worthy.

PART IV: TIME

INVITATION 36:

Rest in Obedience

*"The Peace of Saying
Yes to God"*

"If you are willing and obedient, you shall eat the good of the land." — Isaiah 1:19 (NKJV)

Obedience is often misunderstood as pressure.

As if it's about getting everything right, checking every box, doing every little thing perfectly so God won't be disappointed.

But true obedience? It brings rest — not stress.

PART IV: TIME

It's not about striving, it's about surrender.

When you say yes to God, you're not just following a rule — you're aligning with peace. You're stepping into the flow of His wisdom, His timing, and His way of caring for you.

Even when it's inconvenient. Even when it's scary. Even when no one else understands.

Obedience is trust in motion.

It's faith saying: *"I don't see the whole picture, but I'll move with the One who does."*

And friend, God never asks for obedience without preparing peace on the other side of it.

PART IV: TIME

The Invitation:

Today, don't overthink your yes. Listen for the nudge — then respond:

- 🦋 *Is there something God's been asking you to do — but you've delayed or doubted?*

- 🦋 *Take one step today. Send the email. Make the call. Write the first paragraph. Release the bitterness.*

- 🦋 *Whisper this prayer:*

"Lord, I don't need to understand everything. I just need the courage to obey."

Let that be enough for today.

Why This Matters:

Delayed obedience often disguises itself as caution, but it quietly opens the door to confusion and restlessness. The more we wait to obey, the heavier the decision becomes.

God's voice leads with peace — even when the path is uncertain.

PART IV: TIME

Obedience won't always be easy, but it will always be worth it.

Journal Prompt:

- What is something God is asking me to do in this season?

_____
_____
_____
_____

- What fears or excuses have I used to delay obedience?

_____
_____
_____
_____

- How do I feel after I obey, even in small things?

_____
_____
_____

PART IV: TIME

🦋 What would obedience look like in the next 24 hours?

_____

_____

_____

_____

God's Promises to Carry With You:

"Trust in the Lord with all your heart and lean not on your own understanding." — Proverbs 3:5 (NIV)

"You will go out in joy and be led forth in peace." — Isaiah 55:12a (NIV)

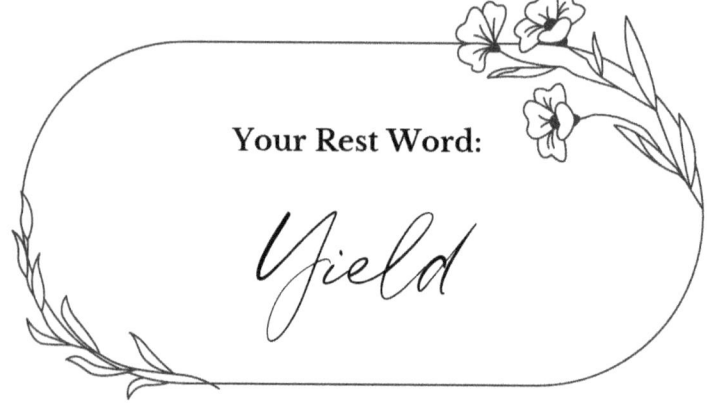

Your Rest Word:

Yield

The road clears when you stop fighting the direction.
Yielding is where obedience meets peace.

PART IV: TIME

INVITATION 37:

Rest in Joy

"Laughter is Still Holy"

"The joy of the Lord is your strength." — Nehemiah 8:10b (NIV)

Joy isn't childish.

It's not a luxury for the carefree or the ones without responsibilities. Joy is a gift. A defense. A spiritual weapon. It guards your mind, renews your heart, and reminds your body what it feels like to breathe.

There's a subtle lie many of us have picked up: *that joy must be earned.*

PART IV: TIME

That we can only laugh after the task is complete, after the healing has come, after the battle is over.

But Scripture shows us a different picture:

Joy doesn't wait for conditions to be perfect — it creates space for peace to flourish in the middle of chaos.

Resting in joy means refusing to put your happiness on hold until life makes sense.

It means noticing the small gifts: the warmth of sunlight, the sound of laughter, the comfort of a memory. It means allowing yourself to delight — without guilt.

God smiles when you smile. He sings over you. And He didn't just give you endurance — **He gave you joy.**

PART IV: TIME

The Invitation:

Let joy be part of your rest today. Try this:

- 🦋 *Play your favorite song and dance in your kitchen.*

- 🦋 *Watch a video that makes you laugh until your belly hurts.*

- 🦋 *Call someone who fills you up.*

- 🦋 *Let joy interrupt the heaviness.*

Declare:

"Joy is not optional. It's holy."

Why This Matters:

Grief and joy are not enemies. You can hold both. But without moments of joy, the soul begins to forget what healing feels like.

Joy doesn't erase sorrow — it anchors you through it. And when you choose joy, even for a moment, you're reminding your body that God still writes beautiful things.

PART IV: TIME

Journal Prompt:

🦋 What brings me pure joy — without obligation or performance?

🦋 When was the last time I laughed freely?

🦋 What memories make me smile just thinking about them?

PART IV: TIME

🦋 How can I invite more lightheartedness into my week?

_____

_____

_____

_____

God's Promises to Carry With You:

> *"You turned my wailing into dancing; You removed my sackcloth and clothed me with joy."* — Psalm 30:11 (NIV)

> *"I have told you this so that My joy may be in you and that your joy may be complete."* — John 15:11 (NIV)

Your Rest Word:

Delight

Joy is not a distraction from the spiritual life
— it's a doorway to it.

PART IV: TIME

INVITATION 38:

Rest When It's Hard to Pray

"When Words Run Dry"

*I*n the same way, the Spirit helps us in our weakness. We do not know what we ought to pray for, but the Spirit Himself intercedes for us..." — Romans 8:26 (NIV)

There are moments when the words just don't come.

You sit in silence, wanting to pray, but your heart feels cloudy. Your thoughts wander. Your spirit is weary. And you wonder — is God still listening?

He is.

PART IV: TIME

Prayer is not a performance. It's presence. It's not measured by eloquence or volume. Some of your most powerful prayers are whispered... or wept.

There are times when the most honest prayer sounds like:
"Lord, I'm here. That's all I have today."

And that's enough.

Resting in God when it's hard to pray doesn't mean you're disconnected. It means you're human.

And even in silence, the Spirit is speaking on your behalf.

Even when your lips are still, your heart still reaches heaven.

PART IV: TIME

The Invitation:

When prayer feels like a struggle, lean into simplicity:

- 🦋 *Sit in stillness with God — no words, just presence.*

- 🦋 *Light a candle and whisper His name.*

- 🦋 *Write one sentence in a journal: "God, I need You."*

- 🦋 *Play instrumental worship and let your tears speak.*

God hears the sighs. The groans. The silent hopes.

You don't have to find the right words — just show up.

PART IV: TIME

Why This Matters:

When we feel pressure to always "pray strong," we forget that God already knows.

Your rest in Him is not based on your ability to articulate. It's based on your belonging to Him.

Sometimes rest looks like silence.
Sometimes intercession sounds like stillness.
Sometimes prayer is simply not walking away.

Journal Prompt:

🦋 What emotions am I holding that feel too heavy to name?

_____
_____
_____

🦋 Have I been judging myself for how I pray?

_____
_____
_____

PART IV: TIME

🦋 What helps me feel God's nearness when I can't find the words?

_____
_____
_____
_____
_____

🦋 How can I practice presence over performance in my prayer life?

_____
_____
_____
_____
_____

God's Promises to Carry With You:

"The Lord is near to the brokenhearted and saves the crushed in spirit." — Psalm 34:18 (ESV)

"Before they call I will answer; while they are still speaking I will hear." — Isaiah 65:24 (NIV)

PART IV: TIME

Your Rest Word:

Presence

Even when the words fail,
God's presence never does.

PART IV: TIME

INVITATION 39:

*Rest in Obedience —
"When You're Tired of Starting Over"*

*"Delayed obedience still
drains your peace."*

There's a certain weariness that comes not from overworking, but from circling the same mountain over and over. You start something, then stop. You commit, then retreat. You know what God said, but the follow-through feels heavy — and if you're honest, fear, doubt, or even convenience keep getting in the way.

It's not that you're rebellious. It's that you're tired. Tired of

PART IV: TIME

trying to obey and not seeing quick results. Tired of being misunderstood. Tired of wondering if what you're building matters to anyone but you and God.

But here's the truth: **nothing wears the soul down like partial obedience.**

Delayed obedience doesn't give you peace — it only gives you time to second-guess. Every time you hold back on what God told you to do, you forfeit a bit of the rest that comes from trusting Him fully.

You weren't created to carry the burden of hesitation. You were called to walk in the peace that comes from moving forward — even when it's uncomfortable, even when it's quiet.

I've been in that place where I knew what to do, but the weight of past failures made it hard to begin again. I prayed, waited for another confirmation, looked for a sign. But God had already spoken. What I needed wasn't another word — it was a willing heart.

And when I finally obeyed? **The peace came. Not because the work was easy. But because the war within me had ended.**

PART IV: TIME

The Invitation:

Today, ask yourself: *What has God already asked me to do... that I'm still waiting to start or complete?*

Then take one step forward. Just one.

- *Make the phone call.*
- *Write the outline.*
- *Send the email.*
- *Finish the thing you've been circling.*

Obedience isn't about perfection — it's about momentum in the right direction.

Why This Matters:

Your rest is connected to your obedience. Every act of obedience builds spiritual stamina. Every small "yes" leads to a settled heart. And when you walk in alignment, you don't have to carry the pressure of outcomes — just the posture of trust.

God doesn't call you to do it all in one day. He simply calls you to follow, one obedient step at a time.

PART IV: TIME

Journal Prompt:

🦋 What have I delayed that God already told me to do?

🦋 How has procrastination affected my peace?

🦋 What fears or thoughts are holding me back from full obedience?

PART IV: TIME

🦋 What would progress — not perfection — look like this week?

_____

_____

_____

_____

God's Promises to Carry With You:

"If you are willing and obedient, you shall eat the good of the land." — Isaiah 1:19 (ESV)

"Commit your way to the Lord; trust in Him, and He will act." — Psalm 37:5 (CSB)

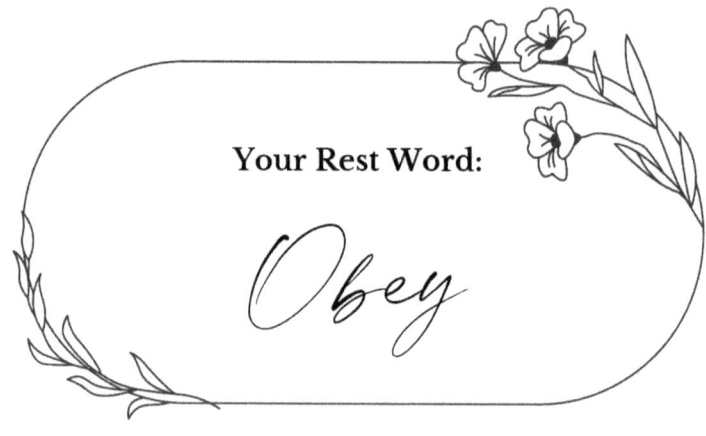

Your Rest Word:

Obey

Obeying brings alignment,
and alignment brings rest.

PART IV: TIME

INVITATION 40:

*Rest in Simplicity —
"You Don't Need to Make It
Complicated to Make It Holy"*

> *"God is not impressed by how busy
> you are, He's present in how
> surrendered you are."*

We've learned to measure value by complexity. The longer the prayer, the deeper it must be. The busier the schedule, the more productive the day must have been. The more intense the effort, the more spiritual the result, right?

Not quite.

PART IV: TIME

God isn't asking for your performance; He's offering His presence. And His presence doesn't require a production. Sometimes, the most sacred rest comes in the smallest, simplest places:

A whispered prayer.
A quiet moment of stillness.
A short walk outside without your phone.

It's easy to believe that rest has to be big and structured — a full Sabbath day, a detailed retreat, a long devotional. But what if the invitation today is to return to simple?

Simple rest.
Simple faith.
Simple joy.
Simple obedience.

I used to feel guilty when I didn't follow a full morning routine. If I didn't journal, pray aloud, read a full chapter of the Bible, and write a reflection, it felt like I hadn't "really" spent time with God. But I've learned something:

God meets us in simplicity.

He's in the breath prayer while driving.
The pause before replying to a text.
The one verse that speaks louder than a whole sermon.

Rest isn't about how much you do. It's about how present you are.

The Invitation:

Today, practice one act of simple rest:

- *Sit still for 3 minutes with your eyes closed.*
- *Write one sentence of gratitude.*
- *Say a one-line prayer and breathe deeply.*

Let it be enough.

Let it be holy.

Why This Matters:

Complication leads to burnout. Simplicity opens the door for intimacy. When you strip away the performance, what's left is pure connection. And that — not your effort — is what restores your soul.

Simplicity isn't lack. It's clarity.

It's not laziness. It's trust.

PART IV: TIME

Journal Prompt:

🦋 Where have I made rest or spiritual connection more complicated than it needs to be?

_____
_____
_____
_____

🦋 What does simplicity look like in this season of my life?

_____
_____
_____
_____

🦋 How can I create space for quiet moments without guilt?

_____
_____
_____
_____

PART IV: TIME

🦋 What would it feel like to believe that "less" can still be sacred?

_____

_____

_____

_____

God's Promises to Carry With You:

"In repentance and rest is your salvation, in quietness and trust is your strength..." — Isaiah 30:15 (NIV)

"Be still, and know that I am God..." — Psalm 46:10 (NIV)

Your Rest Word:

Simple

Rest doesn't need to be perfect
— it just needs to be present.

ABOUT THE
Author

ABOUT THE AUTHOR

Dr. Renee Sunday, MD

The Kingdom and Legacy Builder

Dr. Renee Sunday, MD, is internationally recognized as The Kingdom and Legacy Builder—a prophetic voice, powerhouse mentor, and anointed business architect called to disrupt the marketplace for the glory of God.

A trailblazer in both medicine and ministry, Dr. Renee transitioned from a successful career as an anesthesiologist to become a global force in faith-based entrepreneurship.

ABOUT THE AUTHOR

Through her signature framework, Business & Blessed, she equips high-impact leaders to:

- Align their divine purpose with scalable profit
- Build legacy systems that outlast them
- Serve boldly in both the church and the boardroom

Dr. Renee is the host of the internationally streamed Good Deeds Radio & TV Show, a multi-time best-selling author, and an award-winning publisher. But beyond the platforms and programs, she is a servant-leader devoted to healing hearts, igniting callings, and elevating Kingdom influence.

Her voice carries prophetic weight. Her strategies deliver measurable results. And her mission is urgent:

To raise up a generation of Kingdom CEOs who build legacies, break cycles, and blaze trails that Heaven celebrates.

ABOUT THE AUTHOR

Connect with Dr. Renee:

🌐 DrReneeSunday.com

📱 IG / FB / YouTube: @DrReneeSunday

📖 Join the movement: www.BusinessAndBlessedBook.com

✉️ Book her to speak, mentor, or host: info@DrReneeSunday.com

Notes

NOTES

NOTES

Notes:

NOTES

NOTES

NOTES

Notes:

NOTES

NOTES

NOTES

Notes:

NOTES

NOTES

www.ingramcontent.com/pod-product-compliance
Lightning Source LLC
Chambersburg PA
CBHW050859160426
43194CB00011B/2217